Cambridge Elements

Elements in Ethics
edited by
Ben Eggleston
University of Kansas
Dale E. Miller
Old Dominion University, Virginia

FEMINIST ETHICS

Anita M. Superson
University of Kentucky

CAMBRIDGE
UNIVERSITY PRESS

Shaftesbury Road, Cambridge CB2 8EA, United Kingdom

One Liberty Plaza, 20th Floor, New York, NY 10006, USA

477 Williamstown Road, Port Melbourne, VIC 3207, Australia

314–321, 3rd Floor, Plot 3, Splendor Forum, Jasola District Centre,
New Delhi – 110025, India

103 Penang Road, #05–06/07, Visioncrest Commercial, Singapore 238467

Cambridge University Press is part of Cambridge University Press & Assessment,
a department of the University of Cambridge.

We share the University's mission to contribute to society through the pursuit of
education, learning and research at the highest international levels of excellence.

www.cambridge.org
Information on this title: www.cambridge.org/9781009507202

DOI: 10.1017/9781108587839

© Anita M. Superson 2024

When citing this work, please include a reference to the DOI 10.1017/9781108587839

First published 2024

A catalogue record for this publication is available from the British Library.

ISBN 978-1-009-50720-2 Hardback
ISBN 978-1-108-70632-2 Paperback
ISSN 2516-4031 (online)
ISSN 2516-4023 (print)

Feminist Ethics

Elements in Ethics

DOI: 10.1017/9781108587839
First published online: March 2024

Anita M. Superson
University of Kentucky

Author for correspondence: Anita M. Superson, superson@uky.edu

Abstract: *Feminist Ethics* provides an overview of feminist contributions to normative ethics, moral psychology, and metaethics. It argues that through their criticisms of traditional ethics and proposals for changes, feminists are advancing 'robust agency,' an account of ideal moral and rational agency that promises to give us better responses than those given in traditional ethics to problems in ethics, including how we know our duties, the kind of persons we should strive to become, and why we should act morally.

Keywords: robust agency, feminist metaethics, feminist moral psychology, feminist normative ethics, oppression

ISBNs: 9781009507202 (HB), 9781108706322 (PB), 9781108587839 (OC)
ISSNs: 2516-4031 (online), 2516-4023 (print)

Contents

1 Introduction

If there is a groundbreaking yet still burgeoning area of feminist philosophy, it is that of feminist ethics. Since about the 1980s, feminist philosophers have made significant contributions to all areas of ethics, including normative ethics, moral psychology, metaethics, and applied ethics. They have critiqued traditional moral theories, modified some of them to address feminist concerns, and borrowed concepts from them to serve feminist aims. They have examined the influence of women's oppression on people's psychology, moral character, and actions. To a lesser extent, they have challenged traditional issues in metaethics from the perspective of feminism. Finally, they have addressed topics in applied ethics, such as abortion, adoption, beauty standards, divorce, male socialization, marriage, pornography, pregnancy, post-menopausal pregnancy, prostitution, rape, sex, sexist language, surrogacy, rape, and woman-battering. Such issues either heretofore had not been addressed by philosophers or were addressed but not from a feminist perspective. Yet these issues affect women primarily and detrimentally and call out for philosophical analysis not only in their own right but to highlight their role in maintaining women's oppression. Moreover, feminists complain that women's experiences have largely been left out of philosophy, likely due to the paucity of women in the field. They often import personal experience to their philosophical analysis which not only makes the issues come alive but aids the reader in taking the perspective of the oppressed. Due to space limitations, I will use examples where appropriate to illustrate feminist insights relevant to normative ethics, moral psychology, or metaethics.

It bears mentioning at the outset that the feminist contribution to ethics is not to be equated with a "woman's way" of doing ethics, or a female way of reasoning, or gender essentialism – the view that "all women, in virtue of being women, share a common gendered subjectivity" – as some early work on the ethic of care, a theory initially put forward as a feminist theory, may have suggested (Calhoun, 2004: 8). Feminists largely dismiss the genderization of traits since they believe that it stigmatizes women and perpetuates their oppression. They have come to distinguish *feminine* ethics, which might endorse these tenets, from *feminist* ethics, which is ethics that has as its aim ending women's oppression. One goal of this book is to focus on feminist critiques of traditional ethics and the contributions that feminists have made to ethics with an eye toward ending women's oppression.

A survey of the literature in feminist ethics reveals that through their criticisms of traditional ethics and proposals for change, feminists are advancing a view of moral and rational agency that is at once grounded in and reflective of women's oppression and yet untainted by it. While criticizing and proposing modifications to ethics, feminists are developing an account of ideal moral and rational agency that is even more nuanced than that found in traditional ethics. Some of the features of agency that have been highlighted in the literature include the following: the ideal agent understands the complexities of morality, is able to know what morality demands in a variety of circumstances, appreciates another person's perspective, is autonomous, especially in terms of her desires, bears responsibility for her actions, and sees that she and others have reasons for acting morally that are related to their own interests that the agent cares about and asserts and protects. The unique insight that feminists have contributed to these features of this feminist ideal agency, aside from their connection to women's oppression, is the role that emotion plays in their development. Largely, it has been the case that throughout the history of philosophy, including ethics, emotions have been downplayed in favor of reason, which feminists have argued is due to the historical association of emotion with women and reason with men. Given the addition of emotion, the account of agency emerging from feminist ethics is much richer than that found in traditional ethics. I will call it "robust agency" rather than "ideal agency," since ideal theory has been criticized by feminists as representing only the experiences of the dominant group due to its failure to attend to social context (Mills, 2005: 168). Robust agency might be able to give us better responses than those given in traditional ethics to problems in ethics, including how we know what our duties are, what kind of person we should strive to become, and why we should act morally. The second goal of this book is to elucidate some of the details of what I take to be an emerging account of moral and rational agency.

2 Normative Ethics

Normative ethics is concerned with the issues of how we should act, morally speaking, and what kind of persons we should become. Feminist ethics takes up these concerns with the goal of ending women's oppression. Feminists have criticized traditional moral theory for the ways it has or might contribute to women's oppression. In response, they have offered modifications of these theories, proposed a new theory, the ethic of care, and borrowed concepts from traditional moral theory to employ for feminist aims.

2.1 Feminist Critiques of Traditional Moral Theories

Philosophers need not be feminists to notice some of the jarring beliefs about women held by key figures in the history of philosophy. Since the field had been predominantly – indeed, almost exclusively – male until the end of the twentieth century, these views were likely not discussed much or dismissed because the sexism of these philosophers was attributed to their being products of their time. When more women entered the field of philosophy, it became harder to put aside these views. As you can imagine, many women who read the relevant passages for the first time felt excluded by their philosophical heroes. There was discussion about whether to ignore the sexist passages and whether ignoring them was even possible if they formed part of the bedrock of a philosopher's theory. Feminist philosophers who specialized in the history of philosophy revealed the passages, sometimes found in more obscure works, and challenged them head-on. They criticized many historical philosophers for their explicit or implicit sexist views, showing how the views either excluded women from their theories or assigned them to subordinate roles. One of their main objections is that some philosophers have ignored or downplayed the role of emotions and played up the role of reason because of the historical association of emotions with women and reason with men. Let us illustrate some of the feminist criticisms by focusing on the moral theories of Aristotle, Immanuel Kant, and Thomas Hobbes.

The root of the division between men and women, and reason and emotion, can be traced at least to Aristotle, who wrote his main works in ethics around 350 BC. Aristotle is known for his virtue theory, according to which a person should follow the dictates of reason and aim for the mean, a virtue, that lies between two extremes, the vices of excess and deficiency. Although not all virtues and vices are depicted neatly this way, courage is a clear example that lies between the vices of foolhardiness and cowardice. For Aristotle, a person uses their deliberative faculties to choose virtue over vice. There is nothing at odds with feminism on this simplistic picture of Aristotle's virtue theory, but Aristotle also believes that women should be excluded from virtue because they are not perfect deliberators, a belief grounded in his archaic biological view that women do not generate as much heat as men do, which makes men intellectually superior. Aristotle believes that heat "concocts" matter, and that male semen generates more heat than female semen, or, menses. Women turn out to be "mutilated" males who are physically and intellectually weaker than men (Tuana, 1992: 23–26). However, Aristotle is not an essentialist because he denies that all men are superior to all women. Men and women natural slaves lack a deliberative faculty, which makes free women superior to male and female slaves. Nevertheless, Aristotle believes that women's inferior deliberative capacity requires that they be ruled by a man – free women should be ruled by a husband, slave women by a master. The ruling man can direct them away from passion, which they naturally tend to, and toward virtuous action. On their own, women are incapable of choosing virtue. Their deficiency relegates them to stereotypically sexist roles: they must be obedient to a virtuous man either as his wife or as his slave and must bear and nurture his children. The gendered dichotomy between reason and emotion, together with Aristotle's views about biology, render his theory inherently sexist and incapable of being modified to accommodate feminist concerns.

Feminists have criticized Kant's moral theory also because it downplays the significance of emotion while associating it with women, with the effect that women are excluded from full participation in moral theory since at least some of them follow inclination rather than reason. For Kant, the ideal moral act is one that has moral worth, which is to say that it is done both in accordance with duty and for the sake of duty, which is the moral motive. The moral motive is a rational motive because it has duty built into it, and reason gives us our duties. Kant contrasts the moral motive with inclination, such as selfishness. Whether inclination aligns with duty is a matter of luck, but the moral motive will never lead us astray from morality. Although many philosophers understand Kant to say that an act must be completely divorced from inclination for it to have moral worth, this view has been contested on the grounds that inclination can be present so long as the moral motive serves as the act's motivation (Herman, 1981: 359–66). The point to note is that Kant favors reason and a rational motive over inclination or emotion.

One problem with Kant's view for feminism is his belief that women, at least "civilized" or European bourgeoisie women, are not guided by a sense of duty but by their belief that acting wickedly is ugly (Tuana, 1992: 62). This is because Kant believes that their understanding is "beautiful," giving them a strong inborn feeling for all that is beautiful, elegant, and decorated, and sympathy, good-heartedness, and compassion (Tuana, 1992: 62). Men have a "noble" understanding, which allows them to engage in deep meditation and a long-sustained reflection (Tuana, 1992: 62). Non-European women (and men) are not sufficiently developed to possess even a beautiful understanding (Tuana, 1992: 62–63). Kant is not saying that all women are driven by emotion, but that no woman can achieve a noble understanding. Women in general, it seems, cannot act in morally worthy ways since they lack the moral motive, European women because they are believed to be stereotypically emotional rather than rational, and non-European women because they are not sufficiently developed. This view, however, is at odds with one of the fundamental tenets of Kant's moral theory, which is that morality should be "derived from the universal concept of a rational being in general," because moral laws should be binding on all rational beings, and this includes all humans as distinct from nonhuman animals because humans have the capacity for rationality (Tuana, 1992: 59). Kant contradicts himself here, unless he excludes women as rational (Tuana,

1992: 63). But he includes all humans, along with God and the angels, as beings who are capable of rationality, and clearly specifies that men and women are rational beings (Tuana, 1992: 65).

Like Aristotle, Kant assigns women to the gendered roles of wives and mothers (Tuana, 1992: 65). Were they educated in the development of their rational capacities, this would "weaken their charms" which are used on men, and this would inhibit men's development and improvement and refinement of society (Tuana, 1992: 65). Thus, even if some women can develop their rational capacities, they ought not to. Kant's view reveals another inconsistency in his theory. He urges that women be treated merely as a means to the ends of men and society, but he famously states in the Formula of Humanity that you ought to "act in such a way that you treat humanity, whether in your own person or in the person of another, always at the same time as an end and never simply as a means" (Kant, 1981: 36). In the end, for Kant, women are not able to achieve the same moral status as men not because of their inherent inferiority, but because of his beliefs about the roles they should occupy. Were he to stick to his views about universal rationality and the Formula of Humanity, and drop his association of women with emotion, his theory would be more amenable to feminists. As we shall see, feminists employ various aspects of his theory to serve their aims.

Feminists have also criticized historical philosophers for making implicit sexist assumptions such that when their moral theory is played out, it is likely to maintain women's oppression. Hobbes has been a prime target. Hobbes, like Aristotle, emphasizes reason over emotion. He defines reason in terms of maximizing the satisfaction of one's own interests or desires: rationally required actions are those that best promote one's good or self-interest as defined by oneself and measured in terms of the satisfaction of one's desires or interests. Hobbes believes that persons have only instrumental value, which is to say that their value lies with the expectation that they will benefit others in interactions: "The value, or worth of a man, is as of all other things, his price" (Hobbes, 1962: 73). Hobbes's concern was to demonstrate the rationality of acting morally for persons concerned with promoting their own self-interest and for whom it is rational to do so. Starting from the State of Nature, the state without morality and laws, where each person is rational to act self-interestedly, he argues that each person can expect to gain more in the way of peace, security, and the goods of cooperation by agreeing to morality and laws than he can expect to gain in the State of Nature where each is acting in his immediate self-interest (Hobbes, 1962: 105). Rationality requires that each person sacrifice just enough to reap the expected benefits of cooperation, yet still be able to maximize the satisfaction of his interests.

The feminist complaints against Hobbes are directed at least partly at the model of the Hobbesian agent. For starters, the agent is assumed to be primarily rational, which in effect perpetuates both the association of (white, upper class) men with reason, and women with emotion, and the subsequent sexual division of labor in which (these same) men dominate the intellectual, public sphere, while women are relegated to the private sphere (Jaggar, 1983: 46–47). At best, the appeal to the motive of self-interest construes emotion in a masculine way, as the motive appropriate for prompting actions with strangers in the public sphere with which only men are typically associated (Calhoun, 1988). Moreover, the Hobbesian agent is egoistic, which does not speak to women's experiences that are more about altruism than egoism due to their expectations about caretaking (Jaggar, 1983: 42). The Hobbesian agent knows their own desires, but this fails to acknowledge that sexist socialization can deform women's desires, which, in turn, can perpetuate women's oppression when satisfied. The Hobbesian agent is also abstracted away from his particularities, has needs and interests separate from or in opposition to those of others, and is essentially solitary and overly individualistic (Jaggar, 1983: 41). Not only is this depiction at odds with our human needs and physical dependence on others at least at some point in our lives, it favors the mind over the body. It is at base the Cartesian view of the self as disembodied, asocial, unified, rational, and like all other selves, the epitome of the separation of mind and body, and reason and emotion (Jaggar, 2001: 535). Descartes famously requires that a person separate himself from anything bodily including the senses and emotions in the pursuit of knowledge that can be gained only from reason (Descartes, 1979: 13, 19). Feminists believe that the separation and denigration of the body is largely due to the historical association of women with the body and men with the mind, and that these sexist associations have been perpetuated throughout the history of philosophy because of its endorsement of the Cartesian self. Bodily issues are ignored, the moral code that emerges from an isolated individual who comes up with principles that any rational person would come up with and/or agree to is skewed from reality, self-interest is too heavily favored, and the effects on people's character are likely to be missed, among other things. In sum, Hobbes's theory is problematic because of its focus on reason over emotion and its masculine view of emotion, its heavy individualism and egoism, and its abstraction from social context.

2.2 Feminist Responses

2.2.1 The Ethic of Care

Given the worries about sexism in traditional moral theory, some feminists remain skeptical about the possibility that the theories can be modified in line with feminist aims. In response, they propose an entirely different moral theory, the ethic of care, which has roots in the work of moral psychologist Carol Gilligan (Gilligan, 1982). Gilligan studied Lawrence Kohlberg's work on male subjects and moral reasoning and was curious about whether female subjects used the same reasoning. Kohlberg identified six stages of moral reasoning, with stage one representing selfishness, stage three representing attending to needs and relations, and stage six, the highest stage, representing abstract rules for governing behavior. From her data, Gilligan concluded that for the most part, females used what she called "the care perspective," which emphasizes caring for others, situatedness and attention to details about each other, preserving relations, and satisfying needs, while males largely used "the justice perspective," which emphasizes justice, abstraction from the details of the case, and rule-following (Gilligan, 1982). Females, in other words, were largely at Kohlberg's stage three, while males were largely at stage six. Gilligan's conclusion was not that males were more morally advanced than females, but that there were two perspectives, neither of which is better than the other but is best understood to function like the "duck/rabbit" picture, with each perspective having its own moral concepts and forms of reasoning. Gilligan's work met with a variety of criticisms, including that the differences in male and female reasoning were not significant (Walker, 1993), that they were more likely due to education or general cognitive development than gender (Greeno and Maccoby, 1993), that the sample size and characterizations were inadequate for her conclusions (Luria, 1993), and, most important, that they perpetuated sexist stereotypes about women's reasoning (Tronto, 1993).

These criticisms aside, feminist philosophers seized upon Gilligan's findings to develop a moral theory that would be more in line with (at least white, middle class) women's experiences than men's and that would defeat most of the objections raised about traditional moral theories. Although the details of the ethic of care remain vague, it emphasizes acting in caring ways, but mainly it requires acting from the motive of care, in contrast to traditional theories that favor reason over emotion (Baier, 1987; Calhoun, 1988; Held, 1990; Noddings, 1984; Ruddick, 1980). The emphasis on the motive of care reflects the motive appropriate for raising children, a historically women's role, thereby reflecting women's experiences. Caring lies in contrast with the motive of self-interest that governs interactions with strangers in the public domain with which men are associated. Caring makes us see persons in terms of their particularities and needs, rather than as abstract, independent individuals whose history is unknown and irrelevant to morality and whose value is merely instrumental. The ethic of care is situationist because it enjoins us to use the mother–child relationship as a model for how to respond in terms of another's particularities;

it does not codify our obligations in the way that justice theories do. These differences between care and justice theories are radical and led some feminists to believe that we should altogether replace justice theories with an ethic of care (Gilligan, 1982, 1987; Noddings, 1984; Ruddick, 1980), while others favored incorporating care into justice theories because they saw the importance of each (Blum, 1988; Flanagan and Jackson, 1987; Friedman, 1987; Tronto, 1993).

The ethic of care was in its nascent stages of development when it came under heavy criticism from feminist philosophers themselves. The most damning criticism was that the theory might perpetuate women's oppression by leaving unchallenged, or even valorizing, the view that women are essentially emotional beings, and men, rational (Hoagland, 1991: 256). The paramount goal of a feminist moral theory is to end, not perpetuate, women's oppression (Tronto, 1993: 241–47; Tuana, 1992: 115–16). This remains a point of controversy among feminists. Care ethicists believe that including women's experiences in moral theory is essential for the goal of ending women's oppression. They believe that we need to recognize women's experiences to see what has gone wrong and how to right the wrongs. Critics agree that including women's experiences in moral theory is important but insist that feminists have a critical eye about doing so since the goal is to have a moral theory that aims to end women's oppression. Other objections to the ethic of care include the following: it is grounded in an unequal relationship of a mother caring for especially a male child when the care is never reciprocated (Hoagland, 1991: 253–54); it admits dependency and sharing or losing control, thereby perpetuating women's oppression, in contrast to male caring that has to do with material forms of help (Friedman, 1993: 175, 177); it can be autonomy-denying for women by making women judge their success in terms of the success of their children and lose touch with their own needs (Blum et al., 1973–74: 231–32, 235, 239); and that women's caring is misplaced gratitude to men who either have the power to abuse them or to offer women the privilege of service in exchange for "protection" (Card, 1993: 216).

Worry about such criticisms quelled excitement about a promising new moral theory and replaced it with abundant caution. Indeed, it is fair to say that these concerns almost halted its development in its tracks. Aside from a few feminists (e.g., Kittay, 1999; Held, 2006), most feminists have turned away from the theory at least as a wholesale replacement of traditional justice theories, with the result that it has remained relatively underdeveloped. Yet this is not to say that feminists have abandoned some of the insights of the ethic of care. Some, together with nonfeminists, have insisted that morality pay much more attention to emotions than it has (Railton, 1984; Stocker, 1976). Some believe that rules in morality cannot capture all the moral situations we face or offer conflicting or nonintuitive guidance (McDowell, 1978, 1979) and they might laud the ethic of care for moving morality in this direction. Section 4.3 highlights an important lesson we can draw from the ethic of care, which is that emotion, particularly the motive of care, plays a significant role in how we come to know our moral duties.

2.2.2 Revising Traditional Moral Theories

While some feminists turned to the ethic of care in response to the criticisms made against traditional moral theories, others sought to revise these theories with an eye toward ending women's oppression. Feminists have made two main kinds of revisions: (1) amending the theory itself to make it responsive to women's oppression, and (2) using insights from the theory for feminist aims.

Oppression

Feminists charge that traditional moral theories do not consider the effect of oppression on a person's social situation, nor do they take steps to remedy it. Traditional moral theorists respond that if everyone followed the moral code their theory offers, oppression would not exist. Their theories are generated from the ground up, in the absence of unjust conditions. This is ideal moral theory. Feminists object to ideal moral theory. They claim that oppression exists and that we are socially embedded beings, not abstract individuals with no history, and that moral theory should not abstract away from the features of ourselves that have been tainted by oppression or domination. Failing to acknowledge our social position risks perpetuating oppression when the tenets of a moral theory are applied to persons in the real world. For instance, consequentialism says to maximize the overall good, but if the benefit men reap from women's oppression is greater than the harm women experience, then maintaining women's oppression is morally required. Our moral theories need to recognize and be responsive to our situatedness.

About the same time that feminists began criticizing traditional moral theory for leaving out feminist concerns, they offered independent analyses of the concept of oppression which had largely been ignored in traditional philosophy except for Marx's analysis of class oppression. The earliest, now landmark, paper compares women's oppression to a bird trapped in a cage, where the intersecting wires of the cage are analogized to the interrelated forces of oppression that jointly function to keep a social group subordinate (Frye, 1983). These forces include economics, religion, cultural and social practices, legal and political systems, and stereotypes. Oppression is a difficult concept to understand due to its complexity, the fact that it is often masked, and the fact that people often take a myopic view, seeing only one line at a time on the cage of oppression. One takes a myopic view if, for instance, one believes that women's oppression will end if women have pay equity. Feminists urge that we understand oppression macroscopically, to see how the lines or forces are interconnected in ways that make it hard for the trapped bird or social group to dismantle the entire cage or system. To illustrate the interconnectedness between the forces of oppression, consider how economics and stereotyping can mutually affect each other and prevent women from escaping their oppression. Suppose that a couple harbors no sexist beliefs about labor but wants their children to be raised by a stay-at-home parent (Cudd, 1988). Given the gendered wage gap, the couple decides that it is best for their family if the woman stays home to raise the children while the man enters the paid labor force. But if enough women decide likewise, employers are likely to stereotype women as unreliable wage workers who put family first and pay them less than men for equal work. But this is exactly what drives the couple to choose as it did. Stereotypes and economic disparity are forces that function jointly to maintain women's oppression and would need to be dismantled jointly alongside the other forces.

Feminists have now offered complex analyses of oppression to help explain its existence and how it is maintained by these forces (see Cudd, 2006). They describe in detail the direct and indirect material and psychological forces used by groups to harm other groups (Cudd, 2006: 26). The material forces of oppression include violence and economic deprivation, which are found in all oppressed groups. Violence is direct when it takes the form of physical force against a person, and indirect when it takes the form of threats of future violence, such as the threat of rape of women. Psychological oppression takes direct and indirect forms too: direct forms include terror, humiliation and degradation, and objectification, while indirect forms include false consciousness and deformed desires. A feminist moral theory would deem all these forces of oppression and ways to be oppressed to be morally wrong and aim to eliminate them.

Feminists have also expanded on the notion of oppression in at least two ways. First, they have analyzed the corresponding notion of privilege, and shown how it affects moral character. Privilege is described as unearned assets or benefits conferred systematically to almost all members of a privileged group (Bailey, 1998). Privilege functions like a wild card in a poker game that can be called upon in many circumstances to benefit a member of a dominant group, such as when men's time is considered precious, and their authority readily granted. Feminist analyses of issues such as rape and woman-battering show how privilege is embedded in the legal system and our social practices and thus sustains women's oppression (see Estrich, 1993; Teays, 1998). As we shall see, feminists attempt to amend traditional moral theories in ways that ameliorate the effects of privilege.

A second way that feminists have expanded on oppression is to introduce the notion of intersectionality to explain the way that persons can be members of more than one oppressed group, putting them in a unique position of oppression whose features cannot be attributed to their being a member of either of the groups solely. For instance, black women are oppressed in a way not attributable to either their race or gender alone when they are prohibited from braiding their hair by their employers if they have "front desk" positions (Caldwell, 1991). Intersectionality has been analogized to a traffic intersection, a street with roundabouts, and the curdling that happens when making mayonnaise (Crenshaw, 1989; Garry, 2012; Lugones, 1995). These detailed analyses of the complex phenomenon of oppression need to be tapped to improve existent moral theories or to develop new ones, and to revise our view of ideal moral agency.

Virtue Ethics

Given Aristotle's view that the virtuous life is not possible for women because of their biology, we should think that feminists would jettison virtue theory entirely. They do not, since many feminists see the value of virtue theory itself: it does not import an atomistic, rational, self-interest-maximizing view of the self, it does not attempt to codify morality as a set of rules, and it is not limited to interactions in the public sphere. Many feminists see its focus on character development as a good place to introduce vice as an effect of oppression. This explains the recent surge in feminist work in virtue ethics. Feminists cast aside Aristotle's sexist beliefs and rework virtue ethics from the ground up in a way that allows the possibility for women to reach a virtuous ideal. They examine how gender and oppression affect character, what a virtue or a vice is given the reality of oppression, and the connection between moral goodness and the good life. The result is a more complex view of moral agency than that found in traditional virtue theory.

The primary concern of feminists revising virtue theory is to examine the effect of oppression on a person's character (Dillon, 2012; Tessman, 2001, 2005). Unlike traditional virtue ethics, which takes character and its connection to the good life to be central, feminists take power, or, domination and subordination of groups, to be central (Dillon, 2012; Tessman, 2001, 2005). Some suggest that we replace the term "feminist virtue ethics" with the term "critical character theory" to reflect the fact that character is formed in oppressive social contexts (Dillon, 2012: 85). Domination and oppression negatively affect people's characters and prevent them from living full, good lives. Domination and oppression also affect people's responses to these very forces, including whether they acquiesce or resist. Feminists also suggest that repairing character is a necessary condition for repairing social conditions, which is an interesting reversal to the usual feminist focus on practices and institutions (Dillon, 2012: 87). A feminist critical virtue theory needs to be responsive to the reality of power on these points.

Feminists coined the term "burdened virtues" to denote virtues that oppressed and privileged persons have that stand in the way of their own flourishing (Tessman, 2001). For example, the oppressed might internalize their oppression to the extent that it impedes their developing appropriate levels of confidence, or they might internalize stereotypes of oppression, such as when they come to believe that they are inherently nurturing which leads them to become servile (Tessman, 2005: 56, 65). These traits would stand in the way of their having a good life. By the same token, privileged persons, due to their experiences of privilege, might not develop the virtues of being hard-working or courageous. The other-regarding traits they do develop, such as generosity, might be directed only toward other privileged persons, such as when men are generous only toward other men and only with their time (Tessman, 2005: 68). These traits and the absence of good traits would impede having a good life.

Not only virtues but vices are affected by oppression and domination. The privileged might suffer various vices of domination: abusers and rapists exhibit cruelty, indifference, contempt, and arrogance, while those who merely participate in the system of oppression suffer "ordinary vices of domination," including callousness, greed, self-centeredness, dishonesty, cowardice, and lack of compassion, generosity, cooperativeness, and openness to appreciating others (Tessman, 2005: 54–55). Features of privilege, including its "wild card" quality, can foster arrogance because it can lead the privileged to believe falsely that they earned everything they got through their hard work and native intelligence. The fact that society unevenly represents the views, experiences, values, goals, and achievements of the privileged can make them self-centered and indifferent to the needs of the oppressed. Such vices would also impede having a good life. Indeed, feminists argue that full flourishing involves the pursuit of the well-being not only of oneself but also of others, especially those who are made less well-off by one's privilege (Tessman, 2005: 76). Importantly, and in contrast to traditional virtue theory which takes virtue, the ideal, to be prominent, feminist critical virtue theorists make vice central. They note the essential role that vice plays in the following: trying to become a morally good person who leads a life she regards as morally worthy, raising and educating children and shaping the character of loved ones, making decisions about others that require character assessment such as choosing friends and lovers or hiring someone, understanding how vice can distort character and whether these distortions can be corrected, and theorizing and engaging in the eradication of oppression and domination (Dillon, 2012: 91–96).

Feminist critical virtue theorists recognize that character traits have been gendered and aim to reconstrue them with an eye to social context. What is considered to be nice, patient, cheerful, obedient, modest, assertive, diligent, and so on is very different for men than for women. A male professor who asks to be put up for an award is seen as confident, while a female professor who does the same is seen as overly aggressive. A man who is sympathetic is taken to be nice, while a woman is expected to be sympathetic and when she is not, is seen as not nice. Feminist critical virtue theory aims to eliminate sexist character assessments. It also reconceptualizes virtue and vice so that some vices are considered to be virtues when they are practiced by the oppressed as stances of self-respect (Dillon, 2012: 98). Consider a woman departmental administrator who refuses to copy exams and papers for the department members and is judged to be arrogant on traditional virtue theory, but is seen by feminist virtue theorists as standing up for herself against department members who have taken advantage of her services. Feminist critical virtue theory does not take virtue and vice, and flourishing, to be static (Dillon, 2012: 103).

It would be useful to examine how a feminist virtue theory might play out. I will borrow from the literature a feminist virtue analysis of the timely issue of whether women should "flaunt it" (Barnhill, 2012). Consider Madonna, Miley Cyrus, Beyoncé, and many other women music artists who flaunt their sexuality in their dance (Barnhill, 2012). On traditional virtue theory, modesty is a virtue and is the mean between the vices of prudery and immodesty. Conservatives have long believed that women should aim not for the mean, but for prudery in their dress and behavior because they believe that doing so promotes their sexual flourishing (Barnhill, 2012: 117). When a woman is immodest, she presents herself as a sex object. Conservatives believe that objectifying women violates traditional mores. Feminists also object to the image of women as sex objects, but because this image is dehumanizing to women. They also believe, against conservatives, that endorsing prudery is likely to reinforce the division between "good" and "bad" women, blaming women, but not men, who do not conform and who present themselves as sex objects, for bad things such as rape that happen to them.

A common feminist response to conservatism is to allow women complete freedom to dress and act the way they want, unless it brings them harm (see Wolf, 1992). Indeed, some feminists, sometimes called "lipstick" feminists, have been quite keen on individual freedom because they believe that in "flaunting it," women "own" their own sexuality and are thus sexual subjects, not mere sex objects (Barnhill, 2012: 122–23). They know exactly what they are doing, even if they know they are presenting themselves as sexual objects, and they are fine with that. Yet other feminists caution against this response because, first, women might have desires deformed by patriarchy, and second, women who "flaunt it" present themselves as *mere* sexual subjects, not as full persons whose sexuality is just one part of their entire person, which also includes emotion, intellect, humor, and spirituality (Barnhill, 2012: 126). These feminists believe that women cannot ignore the background context of patriarchy within which they act, where women are seen as sexual beings for men's pleasure. To achieve feminist sexual flourishing, it would be good for the woman herself to be seen and to see herself as a whole person, and when women see themselves and present themselves as such, it is good for all women. This is not to deny that men should change and not see women purely in sexual terms. Nor should women never focus on their sexual side; for older women whose sexual side is often ignored, immodesty can be morally called for (Barnhill, 2012). What counts as sexual modesty is different for different women (Barnhill, 2012: 128). This analysis of the virtue of modesty is an application of critical feminist virtue theory in that it considers the ways in which oppression and domination reflect how a trait can be seen as a virtue or a vice and under which conditions, and how oppression can shape character and is responsive to the fact that it does.

A common complaint about virtue theory is that it is difficult to know what a given virtue calls for in a situation since there are no rules to follow. A feminist version of virtue theory complicates matters beyond this: virtue will be nuanced to context, character will be seen in terms of social context, and a person will have to work on overcoming how power has shaped their character and respond in ways that are self-respecting and bring about their own flourishing and that of their social group. The virtuous person will need to have a decent understanding of feminism, or at least recognize that certain behaviors and practices are sexist. Practice will likely be assisted by dialogue. Morality will be much more complex than simply aiming for the mean. Moral agency will follow suit.

Feminist Contractarianism

Another moral theory that has been revised in response to feminist concerns is Hobbesian contractarianism. Recall that feminists have objected to Hobbesian contractarianism at least for its emphasis on individuality and self-interest, rather than seeing persons as having needs, making choices in a social context that affects others, and having emotions that are other-directed. Not all feminists are convinced that these feminist objections are sound ones. Given patriarchal expectations that women be self-sacrificing for their families, wouldn't it be a good thing if morality and rationality required that they be more self-interested? Some feminists have suggested exactly this, arguing that women's being self-interested is empowering to women because it will help prevent their being exploited by others as they typically are under patriarchy (Hampton, 2002). Because of its grounding in self-interest, these feminists believe that Hobbes's theory should not be dismissed, though at the same time they appreciate the feminist complaint that Hobbes takes persons to have merely instrumental value.

According to Hobbesian contractarianism, each person is rationally required to enter and to keep a hypothetical contract with others because it is in their self-interest to do so compared to their being in a state without morality, which Hobbes calls the State of Nature. In this state, persons are equally rational, equally self-interested, equal in the pursuit of the satisfaction of their desires whatever these might be excepting that each has as his strongest desire their own self-preservation, has a right or liberty to everything including the use of another's body, and that goods are scarce. Hobbes believes that persons are rational to pursue the satisfaction of their desires, and when they do, life for all is inevitably "poor, nasty, brutish, and short." Hobbes argues that it is in each person's enlightened self-interest to form a contract with others to give up some of their rights, and thus the satisfaction of some of their desires, so long as others do the same, with the expectation that they can achieve benefits they could not otherwise achieve. These include security, peace, and the material goods of cooperation. For each right they give up, they incur a corresponding obligation not to act in that way – if they give up the right to steal, they incur an obligation not to steal. The set of obligations contracted upon constitutes the true moral code.

All looks good except when we consider that persons do not operate under these hypothetical conditions. Suppose we were to apply this bargaining scheme to the real world, where bargainers are in a social context such as patriarchy. Feminists worry that it will disadvantage women. Consider Carol Gilligan's cases of Amy and Jake, two 11-year-old subjects who instantiate traditional gender stereotypes (Gilligan, 1982). Amy acts the way women are expected to act in a patriarchal society. She reasons from the perspective of care, understanding morality to be a matter of responding to others' needs, not hurting others, and being in service to them. She places the needs of others before her own and is not able to assert herself or let her own interests count. She loses herself in moral dilemmas and even borders on outright servility (Hampton, 2002: 340). In contrast to Amy, Jake acts the way men are expected to act in a patriarchal society. He reasons from the justice perspective, understanding morality as a set of traffic rules that amount to pursuing one's own interests without interfering with others' interests. Jake is insensitive to others' needs and believes that his own self ought to come first (Hampton, 2002: 339). The worry for contractarianism is that it will leave people like Amy – women – open to exploitation, thereby risking perpetuating women's oppression. Given the patriarchal expectation that women concede the satisfaction of their interests to those of others, their interests will not be respected to the extent that men's interests are. Men might not form contracts with women because they can expect to gain more from interactions with only other men who have more to offer than women. Or men might form contracts with women but the contracts will be uneven in the sense that women will have to concede more given their disadvantaged starting point just so they can incur some benefits. Or women might not assert their interests in bargaining schemes because that is not appropriate behavior for a woman. Or women's desires might be deformed by patriarchy, and even if they insist upon their satisfaction, the resulting contract that respects their desires will be one that serves the interests of patriarchy but not those of women.

Despite these worries, some feminists believe that contractarianism is exactly the remedy feminists are looking for: people like Amy need to assert their interests and have them recognized, respected, and satisfied. They suggest that we modify Hobbesian contractarianism to avoid the possibility of exploitation of women. The contract, they insist, needs to provide all persons with the expectation of benefit. One way we might accomplish this is to import the Kantian notion that all persons have intrinsic value rather than instrumental value as Hobbes thought (Hampton, 2002: 344–45). Kant believed that all beings with the capacity for rationality, as evidenced by their having interests, goals, plans, desires, and the like, have intrinsic value and thereby are deserving of respect. They are to be treated as ends in themselves, not as mere means to another's ends. This contrasts with the view that persons have instrumental value, which is to say that their value lies with the fact that another can benefit from them. With the assumption about intrinsic value in place, each bargainer in the contract is in the position to assert her legitimate interests and insist on her own worth if others put forward claims that might treat them as mere means to others' ends. Moreover, this version of contractarianism can apply not only to public interactions but to private relationships, where each party can ask, "Given the fact that we are in this relationship, could both of us reasonably accept the distribution of costs and benefits . . . if it were the subject of informed, unforced agreement in which we think of ourselves as motivated solely by self-interest?" (Hampton, 2002: 351). Thus, a wife would not rationally accept the distribution of costs and benefits when she is burdened with the lion's share of caretaking for their children. Exploitative contracts would be immoral and irrational to enter.

Under Hobbesian contractarianism, the ideal rational and moral agent is one who merely maximizes the satisfaction of their interests, constrained only by the fear of driving away others who provide an expectation of benefit to them. Under the proposed feminist modified contractarianism, moral agency would be much richer. Women would not be excluded from contracts because men do not expect to benefit from them, which would put them outside of contractarian morality entirely and compromise the possibility of full moral agency. They will be included in contracts that respect their intrinsic value as persons, and they will be able to assert their interests and enter and stay only in those contracts that are mutually respectful. They will not fear that their oppression will be maintained by morality and will be able to thrive as moral persons whose character and interests are not ignored or damaged by oppression. They can fully pursue the satisfaction of their interests in mutually respectful ways and without having to fight off their exploitation and oppression. The noose, so to speak, will be off their necks.

Feminism and Kant

To date, feminists have not offered a feminist version of Kant's moral theory. While feminism and Kant's theory would make strange bedfellows given Kant's views about women, feminists find Kant's notion of intrinsic value to be useful in serving feminist aims. We have just seen how intrinsic value might be used to save contractarianism. Intrinsic value has been used in a feminist analysis of rape in a way that can empower rape victims. On a common feminist analysis of rape, the harm of rape lies with its attempt to degrade the victim by violating her worth as a person. Rape conveys the message that a rapist is superior in value to his victim, and indeed, to all women, and as such the rapist can use her at his discretion (Hampton, 1999: 123, 134–35). It is as if the rapist says through his actions that he and people like him can treat his victim and people like her in this way. Rape makes women be seen as victims and thus in need of protection, which in turn feeds the sexist stereotype of women as weak. It would be easy for a rape victim to come to believe that she is lower in worth than the rapist, especially if society downplays the harm of rape or blames the victim. But Kant comes to the rescue because he believes that a person's intrinsic value can never actually be lowered. It can only be "diminished," which means that it has only the appearance of being lowered even if it sends messages of inferiority. Rape cannot degrade the victim's worth despite the message it sends. Rape victims can take solace in this empowering view from Kant.

Kant's notion of intrinsic value also can explain the wrongfulness of sexual objectification, which occurs when a person's sexual parts or sexual functions are separated from the rest of her person and are either reduced to the status of mere instruments or regarded as if they represent the person (Bartky, 1990b: 26). Catcalling is a classic example of objectification that most women have experienced, where the harasser sees the woman as a mere part or body (Bartky, 1990b: 27). Pornography is another example of objectification whose wrongness lies in disrespect for women's intrinsic value. Consider the case of Linda Lovelace, a pornographic film star who is supposed to represent a fictional and real character who autonomously chooses a life satisfying her insatiable desire for throat sex. Feminists assert that her case is representative of what is depicted in hard-core pornography, although "sex-positive" feminists, those who believe that women's choices about sexual activities are matters of personal preference, might recognize that some women choose to be subjects in pornography, though even they insist that women's choices be consensual. Lovelace did not autonomously engage in these acts because her pimp and husband, Charles Traynor, forced her to act these ways through violence, rape, and death threats. Lovelace was silenced, which is a kind of objectification, by having her autonomy violated because the satisfaction of her genuine desires was completely thwarted (Langton, 2009: 231). Since for Kant a being has intrinsic value when it has the capacity for rationality as marked in part by having desires, Lovelace's intrinsic value was disrespected. Pornography also harms women as a group since when the sex portrayed is seen as autonomously chosen by women, all women are silenced (Langton, 2009: 240).

Some feminists have relied on Kant's views about bodily integrity to defend a right to abortion, though Kant does not weigh in on the issue and whether he considers the fetus to be a full-fledged person is unclear (Varden, 2012). Kant believes that there is an analytic relation between the person and the body, that they constitute a necessary unity. Kant believes also that persons have an innate right to freedom, which he defines as the right to set and pursue ends so long as you respect the same right in others. Because we are embodied, our innate right to freedom involves an innate right to our own bodies (Varden, 2012: 37). When we deny someone the right to bodily integrity, we wrong their person. This is the case with restrictive abortion laws, which deny women's bodily integrity. However, we must respect everyone's rights to innate freedom, according to Kant, so the state would have to balance the mother's rights against the fetus's rights, assuming we can show that the fetus is the kind of being that has such rights and at what stage it incurs them. Surely, when the fetus is in an early stage and in cases of rape, the mother's right to bodily integrity takes precedence over the fetus's rights since the fetus uses the mother's body and not the other way around. On this feminist account, the state should "represent each of its citizens, yet no one in particular" (Varden, 2012: 46). How should the state decide whom to represent? One view is that once the fetus has developed into "a unified spatiotemporal being" with minimal capacities for external action initiated by the fetus, the state has the right to enforce abortion restrictions (Varden, 2012: 44–45). Other feminists might find this view to be at odds with the feminist view that the apt comparison for the basis of equal protection under the law is between women and men, not women and fetuses, especially because fetuses occupy women's bodies and not the other way around. That is, women, like men, have bodily integrity, and the fact that only women become pregnant should not be the factor that ultimately results in restrictions on their freedom. The state should protect women's freedom as much as it does men's freedom – this is how it represents each, yet no one in particular. For this reason, the state should not allow any abortion restrictions if it does not restrict men's bodily integrity rights. Regardless of which feminist view one takes, Kant's theory is useful for deciding the important feminist issue of abortion.

Autonomy

The concept of autonomy is important in traditional moral theory. The Hobbesian model of autonomy is construed as self-determination and freedom to pursue the satisfaction of one's interests and desires without interference from others or even in complete isolation from them. John Stuart Mill was both a utilitarian who believed that we ought to maximize the good and a liberal who believed in people's freedom to make their own choices so long as they do not harm others. For Kant, autonomy is about each of us willing maxims that we could not only impose on others but on ourselves. Feminists have relied on these rather individualistic accounts of autonomy to argue that certain actions are wrong because they are violations of women's autonomy, especially when men are readily accorded a right to autonomy.

Another feminist complaint against traditional moral theory is that it ignores bodily autonomy and related duties. Feminists have discussed women's right to bodily autonomy in the context of abortion, enforced Caesarean sections, maternal-fetal conflicts such as drug and alcohol abuse, pregnancy, surrogacy, sex-reassignment surgery, and rape and date rape. Some feminists have analyzed the notion of bodily autonomy (Mackenzie, 2001; Superson, 2014), but given its significance in feminism, this is an area that welcomes feminist development. One issue is whether bodily autonomy is more than, or different from, being self-determining about one's body by satisfying one's interests and desires relating to one's body. A standard feminist analysis about rape explains it to be an act against a person's will in that it disrespects her desires or interests about the treatment of her body about whether to have sex, with whom, and under which conditions. An alternative feminist account of rape explains that all of a person's interests are interests of her as a person and need to be seen in this way rather than in isolation. Rape turns out not to be just a matter of ignoring, discounting, or thwarting a person's interests about her body, but a violation of her very person, through her body, and as such it is a violation of her bodily integrity. Rape is about how one's whole person is treated and sends a message that the person is a kind of being whose interests – any and all of them – do not count (Superson, 2014: 312).

Another feminist complaint about traditional models of autonomy is that they fall short of addressing feminist concerns in full. Individual accounts of autonomy take the agent's desires at face value – what they are, how they came about – and construe the autonomous agent as one who best satisfies them. Feminists find this account to be too simple and not nuanced to social context. They propose an alternative conception of autonomy that they call "relational autonomy," which is an "umbrella term" of perspectives of autonomy that have in common the view that persons are socially embedded, and their identities are formed within the context of social relationships and shaped by intersecting social determinants such as race, class, gender, and ethnicity (Mackenzie and Stoljar, 2000: 4). On a relational autonomy account, a person is seen not just as a rational being, but also as emotional, embodied, desiring, creative, and feeling (Mackenzie and Stoljar, 2000: 21). It recognizes that a person can be a product of their own oppression and make choices from within that background that might inhibit their self-direction. Perhaps the earliest relational autonomy theorist was Mill, whose work in *On Liberty* and his essay, *The Subjection of Women*, were influenced by Harriet Taylor Mill, a strident feminist who was his lifelong intellectual companion (Mill, 1978, 1869). Mill recognized that women's desires are shaped by patriarchy and that it is difficult to decide whether to respect women's choices when doing so is not likely to promote their own good or the greater good. I will discuss deformed desires in Section 3.1.

3 Moral Psychology

Moral psychology is the study of agents' motivations for their actions. It concerns issues such as what does and what should prompt our actions, why we act or do not act in morally required ways, whether our actions are under our control, and whether and to what extent we are morally responsible for our actions. Feminist moral psychology is concerned with these same issues but from a feminist perspective. In particular, it is concerned with the effect of oppressive socialization on an agent's psychology and subsequent actions, as well as accountability for their actions.

3.1 The Effect of Systematic Oppression on the Psychology of the Oppressed

There are many psychological effects of oppression on the victims of oppression. Stereotyping, sexual objectification, cultural domination, violence and the threat of violence, unequal treatment, and social distancing can cause feelings of being incapable, inferior, and worthless (Bartky, 1990b: 25), feelings of humiliation, degradation, shame, loss of trust in others, low self-esteem, and false consciousness (Cudd, 2006: 163–64, 178–79). Arguably, the effect that has captivated the interest of feminists is that of the formation of adaptive preferences or deformed desires, terms used interchangeably in the literature. As their name suggests, adaptive preferences are those that reflect the agent's adaptation to or deformation by unjust circumstances. The significance of deformed desires is that not only can they affect an agent's autonomy, but also her responsibility for her actions.

What are deformed desires, and how do we know that a person's desires are deformed? The concept of a deformed desire was acknowledged some time ago by Mill, but feminist philosophers have elaborated on it since then. Deformed desires or "repressive satisfactions" or "false needs" "fasten us to the established order of domination, for the same system which produces false needs also controls the conditions under which such needs can be satisfied" (Bartky, 1990a: 42). These desires are not truly a person's own, ones they would otherwise choose absent the social constraints. The "sour grapes" phenomenon explains why this is so (Elster, in Nussbaum, 1999a). Suppose that a fox enjoys eating grapes and they are readily in its reach. Suppose that the grapes are then moved up too high for the fox to reach. Rather than be frustrated, the fox will come to believe that grapes are sour and prefer not to eat them. The same phenomenon explains women's adaptive preferences. Suppose that a girl in a patriarchal society wants to become a doctor. It is likely that she has been sent messages that the top jobs are ones that require huge sacrifices, enormous stamina, and remarkable intellect that females lack, that women's value lies primarily with being wives and mothers, and that girls are not good at science and math. Given these messages and other hurdles she must overcome, she is likely to come to prefer to be a nurse rather than a doctor. Thus, one factor that determines whether a person's preferences are adaptive rather than genuine is the conditions under which they are formed – those a person would not have were it not for the social constraints that impede them would be adaptive ones. The conditions are unjust ones, marked by factors such as unequal education, indoctrination into gendered roles, psychological manipulation, fear of advancement into roles that remain unequal and unprotected, denial of autonomy, lack of information or false information, lack of reflection or deliberation about norms, and lack of options and opportunities (Bartky, 1990a: 42; Mill, 1861; Nussbaum, 1999a: 149).

When a person's desires are satisfied, the person typically benefits in some way from their satisfaction. You want to go to a movie, and when you go, you take pleasure in watching it. But things are different for deformed desires. Their satisfaction benefits the unjust system, often to the detriment of their bearer, which is a second identifying feature. When a female student satisfies her desire to date her professor, this typically reinforces the sexist stereotype that women need to be with a powerful man for self-validation. When women are not taken seriously in the pursuit of their careers, men, but not women, benefit. Of course, the student who dates her professor might get undeservedly high grades and an entry into the profession, along with feeling flattered. But the group, women, suffers harm, and the "real" benefits of conformity are enjoyed by men. Similarly, women who satisfy their desire to conform to the "fashion-beauty complex" might acquire an inferior body image and spend a lot of money and time trying to meet ever-changing beauty standards, though they might at the same time feel narcissistic pleasures and get dates with men. But men are the real beneficiaries because they can pursue their careers and succeed in them without being dragged down psychologically and economically in these ways. Deformed desires involve deception, which is a third feature, because they make women believe that they benefit from their satisfaction, when, in fact, it is the system and the members of the dominant group that really benefit.

There is some controversy about whether women have deformed desires, and whether having them has negative consequences for women. Some believe that women's preferences are authentic because they are no longer the product of undemocratic indoctrination and are accounted for by women's having the right to vote (Sommers, in Nussbaum, 1999a: 130–32). Many evolutionary psychologists believe that women who have preferences that follow traditional norms about marriage and having children are employing a "winning human female strategy" that has them follow the norms it takes to find the fittest male mate, withhold sex to get commitment, and exchange fidelity and domestic service for lifelong sustenance (Wilson, 2004: 105–6). Others caution that feminists beg the question in favor of deformed desires if they assume that women act on deformed desires rather than just make the best of a bad situation, which, they believe, empirical evidence demonstrates (Baber, 2007: 122). A woman who stays in an abusive marriage and does not see that her rights are violated might seem to have deformed desires but really prefers a bundle that includes putting up with abuse while she has a home and basic necessities (Baber, 2007: 111; Nussbaum, 2000: 68–69).

Other feminists, especially early radical feminists who were likely exaggerating the influence of patriarchy on women's psychology to capture our attention, speak as if all of women's desires are deformed (Daly, 1978; Dworkin, 1987; MacKinnon, 1987). Later feminists caution that this view depicts women as being "dupes of patriarchy," who completely subscribe to patriarchal norms and practices of their culture. It depicts women as helpless and ignores the fact that many have rebelled against these forces (Narayan, 2002: 418). Many feminists take the middle ground, acknowledging that women have both deformed and nondeformed desires and are constrained to some extent by the external forces of patriarchy. Sorting out the influence of internal and external forces on a woman's psyche and choices is a complex matter. A Sufi Pirzada Muslim woman who veils has a nondeformed desire to be comfortable and not trip and injure herself but has a deformed desire not to appear as sexually available to men, and faces economic, political, and social ramifications for not veiling (Narayan, 2002). A woman who plays out patriarchal traits of coyness and submission and wants to be dominated by men in sex, may deep down really want sex that is communicative and respectful of the partners' desires (Pineau, 1989: 239).

Most feminist philosophers acknowledge that women have at least some deformed desires. Their concern is whether and to what extent they affect a person's ability to make autonomous choices. If the satisfaction of deformed desires really benefits the system of oppression and not the agent, then they do not seem to reflect the agent's self-determination but her subordination to the system and its ends. If they are unchosen because they are adaptive to the agent's opportunities without her awareness or control, then we might be suspicious about their directing the agent's self. Moreover, the more deformed desires a person has, the more likely she is to be under their sway since it may be difficult to counteract deformed desires with nondeformed desires. Not only does acting on deformed desires threaten to compromise a person's autonomy, it contributes to her own and her group's oppression by reinforcing stereotypes and undercutting their opportunities. This possibility raises the issue of women's responsibility for acting on their deformed desires. These are new issues in moral psychology in that they acknowledge the effect of social forces on a person's psychology in virtue of their being members of a social group.

Not all feminists are convinced that deformed desires compromise the agent's autonomy. When a person's nondeformed desires are tied to her own welfare, she might be autonomous. The woman who wants to be dominated by men in sex but who also wants respectful sex is autonomous when she directs herself to satisfy the latter desire because doing so best promotes her own welfare. Pornography models also prefer things that contribute to their own welfare and would choose better options were they available. Their capacity for self-direction itself is not compromised. Of course, a lot depends on how "autonomy" is defined. Some feminists believe that when we construe autonomy liberally, as the state of being a "normal adult" with no serious cognitive or emotional impairments and not subject to literal or outright coercion from others, then as long as one's deformed desires do not seriously impair one, one can be autonomous (Narayan, 2002: 429). A person can make genuine, reflective choices within the constraints of patriarchy. Indeed, sometimes the starkness of patriarchal constraints can cause the person to face head-on the conflict in her desires and choose to act against those constraints (Narayan, 2002). Other feminists dispute that adaptive preference formation is irrational because not autonomous since it can still guide a person's deliberation and give her reasons for action just like other preferences (Bruckner, 2007: 311). The girl in a patriarchal society who comes to prefer being a nurse to being a doctor might not have self-generated desires, but they are still her own and give her reasons to act. If she would endorse her desire upon reflection, then she holds it autonomously even if it was formed nonautonomously (Bruckner, 2007: 319).

One major contribution to the literature from feminism is the application of models of autonomy to adaptive preferences and sexist norms more generally. There are two models to determine whether an agent is autonomous: procedural and constitutive. Procedural accounts of autonomy make no assessment of the content of a person's desires, values, beliefs, and emotional attitudes, but determine autonomy solely on the basis of whether the agent subjects her motivations and actions to the appropriate kind of critical reflection, that is, some procedure that determines whether the desires and the like survive as genuinely the agent's own (Mackenzie and Stoljar, 2000: 13–14). Constitutive accounts of autonomy, in contrast, assess the content of an agent's desires to determine whether they interfere with an agent's self-directiveness.

Some feminists are skeptical about whether procedural accounts can explain how adaptive preferences cannot be autonomous (Stoljar, 2000). One skeptical feminist explains using Kristin Luker's study of women who adopt false and sexist norms about pregnancy and motherhood, such as that it is inappropriate for women to have active sex lives or to plan for and initiate sex and that "real women" get pregnant and bear children, and who take contraceptive risks as a result (Stoljar, 2000: 99). There are some procedural tests we might use to scrutinize their choices. One is whether they weigh the costs and benefits of using contraception. Since they do, they pass as autonomous, but they should not because they risk pregnancy by not taking contraception or taking it incorrectly due to their adaptive preferences. Another procedure is to test whether they are self-deceived in the formation of their desires, and when they are not, they pass as autonomous. But this test might show that they are not deceived in the formation of their desires, yet their desires are influenced by patriarchal norms and thus count against their being autonomous. A third procedure is to test whether their beliefs and desires are internally consistent. They might pass this test, but still be ambivalent about their desires, such as when they seem to understand the risks of not using contraception yet have unprotected sex. This too counts against their autonomy. A fourth test scrutinizes their first-order desire to take a contraceptive risk. It can pass this test but only because this desire is backed by a second-order patriarchal norm about pregnancy and motherhood, which jeopardizes autonomy (Stoljar, 2000: 102–3, 105–7, and 109). The failure of these procedural tests to label the choices of these women as nonautonomous leads some feminists to favor a strong constitutive view of autonomy which assesses the choices and desires themselves as under the sway of patriarchy.

Other feminists believe that procedural accounts of autonomy fare much better than constitutive accounts, but that we just need to find the right one and not prejudge the outcome by letting in our biases. To illustrate, consider a well-known case of the "Deferential Wife," who tends not to form her own interests, but when she does, counts them as less important than her husband's interests, who takes the fact that her husband has preferences and desires to be a conclusive reason for her to act in deference to them, and who believes that women in general should serve their husband and family first (Hill, 1995). She clearly is under the sway of patriarchal norms about a wife's behavior. One procedural test of autonomy that could be used is a "dialogical" one, according to which an autonomous person has an attitude of responsibility for her commitments and for her self, and is prepared to engage in a dialogue with both herself and others (even if hypothetical) with different viewpoints, and to offer justificatory reasons for her own desires and action-guiding commitments (Westlund, 2003). The agent who can offer such reasons counts as autonomous regardless of whether we agree with her desires and commitments. The Deferential Wife, when pressed about her deference, at best answers that being deferential to her husband and family is a woman's proper role. Yet she fails to be answerable for her action-guiding commitments and instead shows that she is tightly gripped by her commitments, so she is not autonomous. In short, she has no justification for why she follows patriarchal norms. To count as autonomous, she needs to give proper uptake to the question of why she is deferential, even if her response is unsophisticated and not the answer we want (e.g., "The Bible tells me to be subservient.") (Westlund, 2003).

Some feminists are skeptical about both substantive and procedural accounts of autonomy (Khader, 2011). Procedural accounts, they claim, inevitably sneak in an objective notion of the good despite their attempts to be neutral, which is a problem particularly for feminists because of the history of others determining women's good for them. Substantive accounts inevitably involve disrespect for cultural diversity. They each lead to faulty autonomy assessments. If these objections are sound, feminists would have to propose an alternative autonomy test.

A moral agent who comes to terms with how her beliefs and desires are formed experiences moral agency at a deeper level than one who fails to examine – and subsequently modify – these features of her self. Feminists bring to the discussion about autonomy an acknowledgment of the impact of oppressive socialization on women's desires, beliefs, and values. Feminists argue that to be autonomous, a person needs to recognize and respond to the influence of patriarchal oppression on her desires, beliefs, and values. A person who meets this challenge has a richer moral agency than she would have on traditional accounts. On either the constitutive or the procedural model of autonomy, autonomy turns out to be a much more complex matter than merely being allowed to pursue the satisfaction of one's desires, since both models scrutinize whether the agent's desires are truly her own.

3.2 The Effect of Systematic Oppression on the Psychology of Oppressors

While the focus of feminist discussion in moral psychology has been how women's oppression affects their desires and subsequent choices, the focus when it comes to men is how oppression affects their character and subsequent behavior. Why do some men act in sexist ways? Rather than engage in armchair psychology, feminist philosophers offer philosophical answers, though there are some nods to psychology along the way.

3.2.1 Domination and Character Traits

One answer to why some men act in sexist ways lies with how oppression distorts a person's character traits. As we have seen, feminist virtue ethicists argue that oppression fosters certain traits in the privileged, including arrogance, self-centeredness, callousness, indifference, social irresponsibility, and denial of responsibility (Dillon, 2012; Superson, 2004; Tessman, 2005). The privileged might have ordinary vices of domination and burdened virtues.

How does privilege distort character? Recall the "wild card" quality of privilege, which is that a privileged person can cash in on their privilege in any situation. Because of this, privilege can open the door to many other benefits, such as being connected to others in a vast network of relationships (Harvey, 1999). This makes privilege cumulative. These features of privilege undergird its omnipresence. Its omnipresence, in turn, allows the privileged to believe that their advantages are owed to them because they earned them by their hard work or natural smarts. These facts facilitate arrogance in many privileged persons (Superson, 2004: 36–37). Additionally, privilege is generally unrecognized by the privileged because they fail to see the connections between their unearned advantages and the harms of oppression. Privilege is seen as the status quo, it is accepted in society and even by victims who are indoctrinated into complicity, and it is hidden in structures. Complacency about one's privilege is a mark of arrogance (Superson, 2004: 38). Self-centeredness is facilitated by cultural domination, which is the idea that a culture expresses the experiences, values, goals, and achievements of the privileged group and interprets events from the perspective of the privileged group as "the truth" (Young, 1988: 285–86). Privileged persons who see their own values and experiences repeatedly and exclusively expressed in the culture can become self-centered and exclude the needs, values, and interests of the oppressed. For instance, men in the paid workforce did not, until recently, recognize the need for maternity and childcare leaves. When the privileged stereotype members of the subordinate group, which is to differentiate themselves from the oppressed in ways that make the privileged seem superior, they facilitate blaming the oppressed for their fate. This in turn facilitates arrogance, indifference to their victims' suffering, and denial of responsibility for their role in the maintenance of their victims' oppression (Superson, 2004: 38).

The character traits that some men develop due to their privilege can issue in sexist acts. The arrogance of a misogynist who believes that he, but no one outside his group, deserves his privilege can lead him to make his victim suffer for the sake of suffering (Superson, 2004: 39–40). Indifference can cause a man who knowingly participates in a system that advantages men at women's expense not to use his position of privilege to bring about change (Superson, 2004: 41). This explanation for sexism is a systematic one since it shows how the system of oppression and domination can distort a person's moral traits in ways that can issue in sexist behavior. But there is a more specific answer about what can happen at the individual level. It is that of male socialization. Where privilege can give males license to act in sexist ways by distorting their character, male socialization is one of the factors that sustains privilege itself. Male socialization, on a feminist analysis, is mainly about enforcing traditional male stereotypes to the behest of traditional female stereotypes. We can think of female stereotypes as a line on the cage of oppression, that is, a force that helps to keep women down. Since privilege is the flipside of oppression, we can think of male stereotypes as a factor of privilege that serves to keep men in the dominant group.

3.2.2 Male Socialization and Stereotypes

One feminist analysis of male socialization emphasizes the role of violence in the "making of manhood." According to this view, there is a code of honor among males requiring them to inflict violence against mostly other males, and dishonoring and shaming those who fail to do so (Gilligan, 1997). When men are shamed, they develop hatred toward others. Shame also causes a "horror of dependency," which is that it is unacceptable for a man to be dependent on anyone. The horror of dependency causes violence (Gilligan, 1997: 237). Men constitute the lion's share of the number of victims of lethal violence, and we have come to see men as objects toward whom it is more acceptable to be physically violent. This is not to say that women are not victims of men's violence; rather, men's violence toward other men gets expressed in lethal ways. A patriarchal society, on this view, equates manhood with violence and the associated stereotypical traits of aggression, strength, and independence, which in turn can issue in sexist acts.

Another feminist analysis of male socialization emphasizes what is referred to as "compulsive masculinity," which is defined as "the compulsion or need to relate to, and at times create, stress or distress as a means of both proving manhood and conferring on boys and men superiority over women and other men" (Beneke, 1997: 36) The idea is for males to conquer stress and pain in ways that women allegedly cannot, making males into "real" men. For instance, training for being a pilot, a traditionally male role, requires having to endure high G's and intense physically induced anxiety while remaining cool and competent. Some societies have encouraged war out of fear that males would otherwise become effeminate. Rites of passage into manhood for boys are cross-cultural, including spear fishing in shark-infested waters of the South Pacific, enduring insults in Latin America, and being subjected to bloody circumcision rites without flinching in East Africa (Beneke, 1997: 44–47). Male bonding occurs in men who successfully pass these tests, and they dominate and degrade women, who are seen as being unable to pass such tests, to bolster their masculinity. But why such resistance to anything womanly? One explanation is grounded in psychoanalysis, particularly, Nancy Chodorow's theory (Beneke, 1997). According to this view, infants in a stereotypical family identify with their mother because she is the one who spends time with them. But young boys come to realize that they will grow up to be men but cannot identify with their father because he is absent from the home. Instead, boys identify with the role of masculinity and repress and resist what they take to be feminine. Whatever we think of this psychoanalytic view, clearly boys are socialized in many societies to conform to male stereotypes that are different from female stereotypes. Sexism is at the base of male socialization since it enjoins males to be anything but womanly (Digby, 2011).

Some feminists compare male socialization to the more intense kind of socialization that is used to train people for the military, especially at prestigious institutions such as the Citadel and the Virginia Military Institute (May, 1998). The training aims to instill traditional male values and to establish a male culture where boys become or prove that they are men. It takes place in stark conditions with a lack of privacy and even beatings, which are believed to engender self-discipline and the right spirit for leadership, character, bonding with fellow sufferers, and to rein in young male aggression. However, when the cadets are led to think of themselves as "rats," not unique persons deserving of respect, their training can backfire and they come to think of women, who are generally portrayed as even less deserving than themselves, as less deserving than rats and beneath contempt (May, 1998: 129). Since they are forbidden from displaying aggression toward the abusive upperclassmen, their aggression can intensify and be directed at their peers or to women in civilian life (May, 1998: 132). Male aggression can also be channeled into intense pursuit of protection and support for family, leading to a "breadwinner" role that is associated with male dominance (May, 1998: 133).

Male stereotypes play out in harmful sexist behavior, as many feminists have noted. The woman-abuser endorses traditional sex roles, believing that the man should be "the master" of the house and that it is the woman's job to satisfy all his needs and wants (Waits, 1993: 193). He has a tremendous need to dominate and control his victim and believes that he has the right to use violence against her to enforce his will (Waits, 1993: 193). The rapist, who comes out on various studies as having a "normal sexual personality" that differs from the normal, well-adjusted male only in having a greater tendency to express violence and rage, endorses stereotypical views about male dominance and female submission (Griffin, 1981: 318). The practice of female genital mutilation, or FGM, which, though typically carried out by female relatives or a midwife, is a norm set by male social leaders. The goal is to diminish or destroy the woman's capacity for sexual enjoyment, making her into a breeding machine to perpetuate her husband's lineage (Asefa, 1998: 98). Even the practice of men's having to open doors for women no matter how burdened men are and how unburdened women are, has the sexist stereotypes built into it that women do not know their own needs and that they are weak (Frye, 1983). These sexist stereotypes have at their base the idea that men are superior in worth, and women, inferior, which explains the separatism that male socialization encourages.

A pressing question is why stereotypical traits run so deep. Have men always been socialized in ways that perpetuate sexist stereotypes and sustain their dominance? Why is it that males and females seem to have been separated into distinct groups since the beginning of time? The answer perhaps lies with the origins of oppression. Why do persons form groups, and why do they identify with them? One account comes from social psychologists who explain the formation of stereotypes which are generalizations we make about persons based on characteristics we believe they share with an identifiable group (Cudd, 2006: 69). One feature of stereotypes is that they group people usually by visible characteristics (e.g., color of skin), which are then used to make inferences that go beyond what is visible and often, the truth, about all members of the group (Cudd, 2006: 69). Cognitive psychologists believe that stereotyping is essential to efficient information processing and that more attention to detail would cost us in terms of survival and propagation. Commonly, stereotypes favor "in-groups," that is, groups to which an individual belongs, and disfavor "out-groups," that is, groups to which an individual does not belong. Apparently, according to experiments in social psychology, it takes very little for persons to identify with a group (e.g., their agreement about the number of dots on a screen), to be motivated by discrimination against those in the out-group, and to positively evaluate the in-group (Cudd, 2006: 71). Consider how we pit people against each other: Northerners versus Southerners, rural versus urban, and Democrat versus Republican. People want to believe good things about themselves and their group, so they stereotype those in the out-group, separating them from the in-group which is made to look superior. Moreover, there have always been human social groups (e.g., tribes) (Cudd, 2006: 73). Gender stereotypes are socially learned at an early age, especially from one's parents (Cudd, 2006: 75). In addition, there is an abundance of evidence that stereotypes are self-fulfilling, thereby making it difficult for the oppressed to fight back. Their internalization, together with the violence and threat of violence that men direct against women, leads feminists to claim that this is why "we have not succeeded in ending the longest standing case of oppression on the planet" (Cudd, 2006: 96).

This is not to suggest that gender is binary, nor that there is no violence against transgender individuals. Indeed, such persons are frequently the targets of violence. According to at least one feminist explanation, violence against transgender persons whose gender presentation or appearance misaligns with their sexed body or concealed reality has its roots in sexist and racist violence and oppression at large (Bettcher, 2007). Transphobic violence, when part of a heterosexual and sexist context where a woman's dress is taken to indicate both her genital status and sexual willingness, might even be seen as justified as a way of putting women back in their place – deceivers about their gender deserve bad treatment, a belief that is intensified by racist stereotypes of black women as "Jezebels" (Bettcher, 2007: 56–57).

3.2.3 Can Sexist Men Change?

These explanations for why the privileged come to act in sexist ways raise the questions of whether the privileged are able to change their characters, and what it would take for them to see the force of their beliefs about and actions directed at the oppressed. Is it a matter of a failure to understand something about those they oppress, or is it that they lack certain emotions? This is a complicated issue that bears on at least three deeper issues. First is the issue of ideal or full moral agency – what it consists in and how we achieve it. Many traditional moral theories depict morality as a set of rules and regulations such that if a person learns these and follows them strictly, they will achieve full moral agency. Morality is purely cognitive. When persons act immorally, their doing so is a failure of cognition: the person did not understand the rules, suffered from weakness of will, did not know the facts of the situation, deliberately flouted the rules, and so on. Feminists who take a lesson from the ethic of care suggest that matters are not so simple. They believe that full moral agency is bereft without emotion, and that emotion is necessary for knowing one's moral duties (Little, 2007). Other philosophers writing without feminist aims believe that emotion is necessary for a full comprehension of morality in all its nuances. A description of the psychopath is useful for seeing what is missing. The psychopath is someone who can understand only simple moral rules and can at best only mimic them because he lacks emotions such as love that are necessary for seeing the complexities of morality (Duff, 1977). For example, to understand how it is wrong to hurt someone, you have to know what it is to hurt someone, and for this you need an understanding of the kinds of interests and concerns people can have (Duff, 1977: 196). On this latter view, the ideal moral and rational person is not one who merely meets the criterion of the expected utility theory by acting in ways that are best for them but is one who can understand the complexities of morality, sees that her own and others' values give them reasons for action, and sees the emotional and moral significance these aspects of life have for others and for himself (Duff, 1977: 192–93). Ideal moral agency on these views has an emotional component alongside a cognitive component. Failures of morality are not merely failures of cognition; cognition and emotion inform each other and are each necessary for a full comprehension of morality.

A second issue is what the privileged need to do to not act in sexist ways. Is there any hope of fixing what patriarchal socialization instills? A common view is that if we present a person with an argument showing that they are irrational about how others should be treated, or show them that some of their beliefs about others are wrong (e.g., the belief that head and jaw size in African Americans is different from that of Caucasians and justifies different treatment, or that women's having a uterus makes them hysterical), this is sufficient for their becoming better moral agents since once they understand the argument, they will be appropriately motivated. Just explain feminism to the uninformed, and they will be on board, is the view. A theoretical issue lurks here, which is that of internalism versus externalism. Internalists about obligations or reasons, and motivations, believe that there is a necessary connection between obligations or reasons, and motivations, such that if one has (or acknowledges that one has) an obligation or a reason to act a certain way, one necessarily has a motivation to act that way. This is just one version of internalism. Externalists deny that there is a necessary connection between these concepts. There is a lot of literature on the internalism/externalism debate in metaethics showcasing the various versions it takes as well as its significance for other issues in ethics (see, for example, Korsgaard, 1986; Smith, 1994; Brink, 1986; Harman, 1975; Copp, 1982) and the standard debates are independent of how this bears on feminism (but see DesAutels, 2004; Superson, 2009). The point here is that in this version of internalism, understanding that one has an obligation or reason to act necessarily entails that one is motivated to act, and we might think that to change an oppressor, we need simply to give him an argument, and that would generate the right motivations, at least if he truly understands (and some would say, "accepts") the argument. Still, a weak version of internalism would say that the person has the right motivation, but only a strong version of internalism would say that this motivation was overriding among his other motivations. And the internalist would have to show that this motivation, even if it is the strongest a person has, must issue in the relevant action. Externalists deny these necessary connections and believe that giving the oppressor an argument would be insufficient for issuing in a change in their actions; reasons can, but do not necessarily, motivate.

Feminists generally have not cast the issue in terms of the internalist/externalist debate. Instead, they move the debate to a practical level, suggesting ways to make the privileged understand the position of the oppressed. One suggestion is to become aware of one's privilege as a knapsack of benefits unjustly bestowed upon one (McIntosh, 1993). Another suggestion is to take the first step of disaffiliating from one's own privilege (Frye, 1995). Websites such as "Teaching Privilege" are available to make the privileged see their own privilege and to access the position of the oppressed. Another tactic feminist philosophers employ is to write from "a personal voice." The reasons they do so are varied but include engaging the moral imagination or feelings of empathy and motivating philosophers to recognize and understand the gravity of harms relating to oppression that were previously ignored or treated superficially. Consider a feminist philosopher's description of the humiliation she experienced when she was the recipient of street sexual harassment, where she is happily bouncing down the street, watching the birds in the trees, when the air suddenly fills with catcalls and whistles that freeze her, make her face flush and her motions become stiff and self-conscious about her body, being made to feel as her harasser wants her to feel (Bartky, 1990b: 27). Another feminist philosopher attempts to distinguish those who make unwelcome sexual advances from those who are gender bullies – the real sexual harassers – by describing her experience in graduate school of her professor who patted her on the rear end in front of her (mostly male) colleagues before class began (Bordo, 1997). Perhaps the most graphic and horrific example comes from a feminist philosopher who describes her own experience of being raped and almost murdered by a stranger in another country, during an hour-and-a-half encounter where she was "grabbed from behind, pulled into the bushes, beaten and sexually assaulted" while on a walk in the peaceful countryside. She was strangled until she lost consciousness, dragged by her feet into a ravine, smashed in the head with a rock, and left for dead (Brison, 1993). In writing from a personal voice, feminists address philosophers, who, in discussing moral theories, write as if they know how being harmed in grievous ways feels and the role this kind of harm should play in deciding our moral obligations, which is an arrogant stance that silences victims (Brison, 1993: 11). Others who do not write from a personal or even feminist perspective use more traditional tools such as analogies to get the privileged to take the perspective of the oppressed. A famous paper on abortion, for instance, uses science-fiction-like examples to get a nonpregnant person to imagine himself or herself to be in the position of a pregnant woman who is considering abortion in the cases of rape, when the mother's life is at stake, and when contraception has failed (Thomson, 1971). They involve being kidnapped and having a famous violinist hooked up to their kidneys for nine months, being trapped in a house with a rapidly growing baby that will crush them to death if no one interferes, and living in a house with fine mesh screens on the windows only to have a people seed drift in and take root in the carpeting and upholstery and grow into a full-fledged person for whom they are responsible.

These feminists are proposing what has been called "world-traveling," defined as "traveling" to the world of others who occupy a different position in the social hierarchy (Lugones, 1995). To world-travel, one needs to give up the arrogant construction of concepts from one's own perspective. To explain the notion of world-traveling, the notion of playfulness is employed: a person finds that in some worlds, she finds that she is playful, but in other worlds, she finds that she is serious. Whether she is playful, or more accurately, is seen as playful, is a matter of how the dominant group constructs the concept of playfulness. Perhaps the privileged can use world-traveling to come to see the nonprivileged as equal in humanity by directing their attention away from themselves and toward the nonprivileged, by appreciating the personhood status of the nonprivileged, and by coming to understand the complex hurts involved in oppression (Superson, 2004: 38–39). World-traveling has the traveler understand not as an observer, but as a real participant in a particular world.

World-traveling, perhaps, is easier said than done. Consider that the oppressed live their lives with omnipresent stereotypes held about them. Practices such as enforced pregnancy, for example, contribute to the image of women as breeders, much like the practice of rape makes us see women as potential rape victims in need of protection (Cudd, 1990). Stereotypes are difficult for an individual to overcome, and even women whose behavior flies in the face of them are often deemed to be exceptions to the rule. How could someone who has not lived in the shadow of negative stereotypes come to understand what it is to go through life with the stereotypes about the oppressed applied to them, and then change their own behavior? Some feminists are skeptical about whether the privileged are capable of world-traveling, or stepping into the shoes of the oppressed, as it were. One explanation is that the privileged cannot imagine how a victim feels because the privileged have different social, and so different emotional, constitutions due to their socialization that makes them experience things differently from the oppressed (Thomas, 1999). Thus, for example, a heterosexual man cannot imagine how a female rape victim feels, since he cannot imagine the general fear of rape that most women have, and he does not have to deal with social attitudes that make women targets of sexual violence (Thomas, 1999). To step into the shoes of women, men would have to be viewed as less than full and equal members of society and have painful memories of these experiences. This is unlikely, according to these feminists. On this view, although we can know the particular instances of sexism as the women philosophers discussed above have graphically related, and we can understand oppression on an intellectual level, if we do not ourselves live it, we will have a different social and emotional constitution which affects our ability to world-travel. Compare being stereotyped to having a serious, chronic illness or disease that affects every aspect of your life and your being. Unless you live with the impairment, it is hard to see the impact it makes on a person's life.

A third issue is what bearing the ability to take another's perspective has on the agent's moral responsibility for not acting in ways that contribute to women's oppression. I address this in the next section.

3.3 Responsibility

3.3.1 Responsibility of Oppressors for Oppression

Typically, when we speak about moral responsibility for one's actions, we are talking about an agent who performs an act that has consequences that are clearly the result of the act. For example, Jill gets mad at Jack and shoots him in the leg and he suffers an injury to his leg. We can identify Jill, Jack, and the harm to Jack's leg and determine Jill's moral responsibility by examining details such as her motives, Jack's role in making Jill mad, and so on. Things are murkier when it comes to responsibility for oppression due to the difficult nature of oppression – it takes subtle forms, it is often normalized which makes contributors and even victims oblivious to it, and it is institutionalized and part of the structures of society which means that it can be carried out independent of anyone's harboring bad attitudes toward the oppressed or acting in ways that directly harm them but by merely participating in the system. On the one hand, a system of oppression can continue without deliberate sexist acts, and without acts done by any particular individuals, which might seem to absolve oppressors from responsibility. On the other hand, certain individuals directly help to ensure that the system is maintained through their actions or inaction. Being ignorant, negligent, or self-deceived are not innocent motives. An additional problem is that separating a person's own sexist behavior from systematic sexism can be difficult. Nevertheless, if no one is deemed responsible for a group's oppression, it is likely to continue.

Feminists have defended a wide range of positions about the responsibility of oppressors for their role in oppression. One of the more lenient positions is that we should excuse a person for moral ignorance when they are in an "abnormal moral context" where only those in a subgroup of society, such as feminists, make advances in moral knowledge faster than they can be disseminated to and assimilated by the general public and groups at risk (Calhoun, 1989: 396). Feminists come up with new terminology (e.g., "marginalize," "the Other") and sophisticated analyses of oppression that the general public cannot be expected to know until these become commonplace. Nevertheless, if we merely excuse those in the dominant group for their ignorance, we seem to condone their behavior, but if we want to motivate them to act in feminist ways, we should reproach them.

Other feminists are less lenient. Why should we absolve from responsibility a person who is influenced by their upbringing in a sexist society when in reality they choose not to know what they can and should know? The suggestion is that it is our moral failings as human beings rather than "cultural limitations" that best explain the role of the privileged in oppression. On this view, the privileged have "affected ignorance." Feminists who hold this view cite as evidence the fact that people often act against cultural norms and even radically revise them through their actions (Moody-Adams, 1994: 296, 305). Cultures persist only because individuals capable of responsible action persist, and though we can be influenced by cultural norms, we can also act against them (Moody-Adams, 1994: 292–93).

Still other feminists believe that not every case of widespread moral ignorance is a case of affected ignorance. Sometimes we lack equal access to the full range of actual and possible moral knowledge, and sometimes moral discoveries have not yet become commonplace (Isaacs, 2011: 163–64). In these cases, we should be excused for acting immorally when our actions are linked with wrongful social practices. Feminists might have certain moral knowledge that they acquire through their experiences, but privileged persons might lack this knowledge since they do not have the same experiences. This view echoes the belief that the privileged are constituted differently from the nonprivileged due to their experiences. Does a lack of experience absolve the privileged from responsibility for knowing and acting in feminist ways? Some feminists suggest that the privileged should practice moral deference, that is, defer to those who speak in an informed way about experiences specific to their social position to which the privileged lack access, and acquire sensitivity to the other's position (Thomas, 1999: 189). Other feminists add that the moral knowers with blind spots due to their privilege have an obligation to become aware of their blind spots and to defer in a way that is epistemically responsible. This involves not simply deferring on the grounds that those in oppressed groups are better positioned to perceive sexism, but attempting to understand the morally salient features that are blocked from one's perceptions (Grasswick, 2012: 326). Granted, the nonprivileged often have difficulty articulating exactly why someone comes across as sexist since sexism can be expressed in subtle ways. It is not uncommon to hear a woman say: "I don't know how to explain it, he just strikes me as sexist." Since the privileged lack the perception and sensitivity especially to subtle sexism, the morally and epistemically required response for them is not to be a lazy knower who simply defers to others but to investigate what they are missing by listening to the testimony of others, engaging with them, and reading about the experiences of others who are situated differently (Grasswick, 2012: 323–28).

Other feminists have much less lenient views about responsibility for the harms of oppression. This is because they believe that even though oppression is a difficult concept to grasp and the privileged might lack the special knowledge that feminists and the oppressed have, the privileged should know the Kantian "basic facts about humanity." This is to say that all persons are equal in some fundamental sense that transcends gender, race, and so on. Immanuel Kant describes the notion of humanity, that all persons have the capacity for rationality and autonomy, and so possess dignity and are deserving of respect. They have intrinsic value in virtue of being persons. This is not a difficult concept to grasp, which leads some feminists to hold responsible those who disrespect others' humanity (Superson, 2004; Zack, 1998). Of course, patriarchy attempts to disguise these facts about women through stereotyping, dissemination of false beliefs, and so on, rendering it difficult to recognize that a particular behavior or practice violates a person's humanity. Responsibility ascriptions might be made on the basis of the degree of difficulty involved in sorting through patriarchal norms to uncover whether a particular behavior or practice violates a person's humanity, but feminists who hold this less lenient view about responsibility likely believe that many of us know when we are disrespecting another's humanity.

Whatever one's view about the moral responsibility of oppressors for oppression, these feminist debates highlight the fact that feminism has presented a more complex view of moral agency than that found in traditional morality. A responsible moral agent must attend to the social position of others that they may have been previously ignorant of, they must become aware of their moral blind spots, listen to the oppressed to grasp their experiences, and tune in to whether they are letting gender stand in the way of respecting someone in virtue of their humanity. In this way, feminism has broadened our understanding of our moral obligations as well as of our moral agency.

3.3.2 Collective Responsibility

As we have seen, oppression is explained by interrelated forces that jointly function to keep a social group subordinate. The nature of oppression raises the possibility that responsibility for oppression may not fall completely on individuals and their direct actions. Women's oppression is maintained not only by individuals who act in sexist ways but systematically through the forces of oppression that have sexism embedded in them. Under patriarchy, economics, religion, cultural and social practices, political and legal systems, and stereotypes all have sexism embedded in them, and sorting out how these forces are interrelated can mask the role of the individual in sustaining oppression. A person who has never been guilty of sexual harassment, rape, or discrimination might insist that he is not responsible for the existence of these practices. Feminists, however, have seized on the notion of collective responsibility, according to which all men are responsible for aspects of women's oppression (May and Strikwerda, 1994). Consider the practice of rape. Some feminists argue that men are collectively responsible for rape because most if not all men contribute to its prevalence (May and Strikwerda, 1994). A patriarchal society promotes a "rape culture," in which men are not strongly discouraged from rape and in which there is an attitude about women that may make many men view rape as unremarkable. Aside from direct perpetrators of rape, who most of the time are responsible for their acts of rape, other men share some responsibility for the prevalence of the practice of rape on this view. These feminists want to hold responsible men who interact with other men in ways that make rape more prevalent in society, such as when they participate in the practice of male bonding. Men who would rape were they given the opportunity where their inhibitions were removed, as well as men who could have prevented other men from raping, share responsibility with actual rapists (May and Strikwerda, 1994: 146). Even men who merely benefit from the existence of rape share some responsibility, since they gain strength from male bonding against a highly sexualized stereotype of the "female," they enjoy freedom of movement that females do not, and they enjoy being in the role of protector while females are made to feel dependent on men for protection against potential rapists (May and Strikwerda, 1994: 147–48). This account shows how a person can share responsibility for harms they do not directly cause. It expands the traditional view of moral agency beyond a person's individual actions: robust moral agency calls for the agent to consider their role in social practices from which they merely benefit but in ways that harm members of oppressed groups, and to respond accordingly.

3.3.3 Responsibility of the Oppressed for Immorality

While social privilege can burden men with collective responsibility, does oppression free women from responsibility for acting immorally? Some race theorists have discussed this issue in terms of racial minorities. One race theorist who aims to free in part individuals from responsibility for immoral actions such as rioting and gang banging argues that social injustice generates economic deprivation for racial minorities, which constantly challenges their self-esteem, causing them to go through stages of resentment, embitterment, and finally moral death (Menkiti, 1977–78: 227–30). Blaming individuals for primarily institutional failures, on this view, is unfair. Though parsing out the causal connection between social injustices and individual immoral actions is difficult, at least this race theorist believes that it makes as much sense to say that society is a culprit as it does to say that there are debts owed to society (Menkiti, 1977–78: 237). Compare this to attributing responsibility to a corporation for its role in climate change or a plane crash. Still, the difficulty lies in tracing responsibility for a person's actions to the social conditions under which the person lives.

The kind of immoral behavior that women tend to engage in, which might be caused by their oppression, is to internalize their oppression, acquire deformed desires, and adopt stereotypical traits and roles such as becoming servile that either violate a duty of self-respect or harm women as a group (see Section 3.3.4). These harms, of course, are different in nature from the harms of gang banging. Feminists need to juggle the notion of absolving women from responsibility due to their social condition, with granting them full moral agency which on the face of it seems to recognize holding women responsible for immoral acts regardless of their social condition. Feminists have proposed agency-protecting ways of absolving women from responsibility when clearly their social condition plays a significant causal role in their actions.

Consider again the case of the Deferential Wife, whose complete devotion to her husband and belief that she is fulfilling her proper role as a woman makes her servile. Kant famously believed that servility is immoral because it violates a duty to be self-respecting. Any rational being, Kant thought, would see himself as an end in itself, which flies in the face of servility.

Feminists complain that Kant's view is too harsh because it does not recognize that the identities of persons like the Deferential Wife have been largely constituted by patriarchy and are incompatible with a conception of themselves as persons (Stark, 1997: 76–77). One feminist proposal is to impose a self-worth condition on responsibility, according to which to be responsible, a person must be and see herself as an eligible participant in moral exchanges involving offering reasons, seeking excuses, begging forgiveness, and blaming (Benson, 2000: 79–85). If a person internalizes oppressive social norms, this can interfere with her regard for her own worth and her sense of responsibility or her accountability to others. She might not see herself as an eligible participant in a community of moral dialogue that requires that she be able to speak for her own agency in response to criticism from others and recognize her own intrinsic worth. When she does not see herself as such, then we should exempt her from responsibility for, say, being non-self-respecting.

Feminists acknowledge that mitigating women's responsibility for behaviors like being deferential risks undermining women's agency. They are loathe to contribute to the damage to women that patriarchy has done in this regard. This might explain why feminists have generally shied away from absolving women from responsibility for certain immoralities. Excusing a person for wrongdoing suggests that she was mentally impaired, not reasonable, or overcome by emotion. Feminists have argued for justifying reasons, rather than excusing reasons, to defend a woman's seemingly immoral actions when they are directly tied to patriarchy. For example, when a woman who is severely and repeatedly abused kills her abuser, we can defend her actions by showing that she responded appropriately given her circumstances and her being able to determine rationally that self-defense was warranted, rather than showing that she was in some way out of her mind (see Teays, 1998: 61–64). Justifying reasons are empowering to agency.

A feminist attempt to offer justifying reasons to defend the Deferential Wife's servility has been offered in response to a well-known, not specifically feminist, attempt to defend the Victim of a Deprived Childhood who was given no love and was beaten by his father and neglected by his mother and later in life embezzles money (Wolf, 1986). On the latter view, there are reasons for the Victim of a Deprived Childhood not to embezzle, grounded in "the True and the Good," but such a person could not have had reason to act morally since his circumstances made him not be able to see that these moral reasons exist. His reasons, in short, are determined by his circumstances. Since his reasons are determined, so are his actions stemming from these reasons. Thus, he is neither blameworthy nor responsible for his immoral actions.

This way of defending a person who is the product of their upbringing has been criticized for being agency-denying, and thus feminists would be cautious in defending a character like the Deferential Wife who is the product of patriarchal socialization on these grounds. An initial, agency-protecting response, one not given in the context of feminism, argues that the Victim of a Deprived Childhood has a justified failure to tell right from wrong – anyone in his circumstances has reason to act the way he does, even though they also have reason not to act immorally (Buss, 1997). To support this conclusion, the case is fleshed out as follows: the Victim as a child came into contact mostly with people who either beat him, supported those who beat him, or ignored his misery. Whenever he was beaten, he was first taunted. Years later, when he is taunted, he hits his taunter. The Victim is not determined by his reasons, and he has a moral reason not to hit his taunter, but he would have to be truly exceptional not to take his past experiences as representative of human nature, much like a person who has been bitten repeatedly by dogs would be truly exceptional to think that the growling dog in her path will not bite her (Buss, 1997: 354). Whether the Victim is justified in hitting his taunter depends on whether he has available alternatives, how unacceptable his action is, and the details of his background. Since he has always been beaten after being taunted, he is justified in hitting his taunter, though hitting is itself morally wrong. We could apply this reasoning to the Deferential Wife: were her circumstances – her socialization – so bad, perhaps because she met up with mostly sexist people who tried to undermine her worth throughout her life, we might say that she is not responsible for her servility, though servility itself is wrong.

A stronger, more agency-empowering response would show that the Deferential Wife's servility is itself justified, not merely that she is justified in being servile, though servility is itself wrong. It would justify her actions themselves, and not offer excusing reasons dependent on either the agent's psychology or her circumstances but would offer justifying reasons that free her from responsibility for being deferential considering her circumstances (Superson, 2010). This account uses the case of Aileen Wuornos, a Florida prostitute who was convicted of and executed for killing seven men who sought sexual "services" from her, and whose story is the subject of the 2003 movie, *Monster.* Wuornos was sexually abused at the age of eight by her father's friend, and when she told her father, he beat her. After years of sexual abuse, she turned to prostitution. When one of her "clients" brutally raped her, she shot him dead, and then shot and killed several other men during attempted acts of prostitution, whether she feared they would rape or kill her. Her first killing was clearly an act of self-defense: she could fight back only by killing him since she was handcuffed to the steering wheel of his car during the attack. She knew that killing in general is wrong, but was furious about the attack, felt helpless about her situation and the way she had been treated all her life and how she expected to be treated were she to file a legal charge, and felt remorse after killing her attacker. Like the gang banger, she has experienced a death of sorts and cries out for self-defense and acts in a way to protect and assert her dignity. When she kills her first "client" in self-defense, her act of killing is itself justified because it is a way of protecting and asserting her dignity and asserting that the attacker has no right to try to take her out of the moral community. In the cases where she kills her other clients, she doubts her dignity and status as a full member of the moral community that grants and protects rights due to the repeated attacks on her dignity. These clients in her mind serve as stark reminders that she is a mere object that can permissibly be sexually abused, and she is unable to separate them from the rapist (Superson, 2010: 268). She is much like the Victim of a Deprived Childhood who believes that taunting will always be followed by a physical assault. Viewed in this way, her acts of killing can be re-described as acts of asserting her worth in defense of a persistent attack on it. They too are acts of self-defense, of defending her worth as a person, and it is from this perspective that such acts are themselves justified. This is what absolves her from responsibility. This account is agency-preserving since it defends the agent with justifying reasons rather than excusing or deterministic reasons (Superson, 2010: 26).

Let us apply the reasoning in this case to that of the Deferential Wife. Like the case of Wuornos, she was sent strong social messages of inferiority causing her to believe that women should serve their families, and that it is self-respecting to do so. Instead of acting in ways that assert her dignity, she acts contrary to this since she is confused about her worth. She acts in ways that she mistakenly believes assert her worth since she believes that the self-respecting way to act is to be servile to her husband and family. She is happy and proud to be servile and thinks she confirms her worth by being servile and believes that all women should be like her. Servility itself is morally wrong, according to Kant, because the servile person treats herself merely as a means to her own ends. Kant believes that the servile person acts out of inclination, but the Deferential Wife acts out of confusion about her worth. Her servility is justified in the sense that it is a legitimate response to her confusion about her worth that results from social messages of inferiority. In both cases, the person's dignity has been attacked and it is not reasonable to expect her not to act to try to assert it and reestablish herself in her own eyes and in the eyes of her attacker and the moral community at large. Their acts of asserting their worth are themselves justified since they are acts of self-defense. This feminist analysis of responsibility for seemingly immoral acts adds complexity to traditional accounts of responsibility because it is responsive to the agent's social context. It is another element in robust agency.

3.3.4 Responsibility for Resisting One's Own Oppression

A topic that has attracted a lot of attention from feminists and is a source of controversy is whether women are responsible for resisting their own oppression, since if they do not, they might contribute to it and harm themselves and women as a group. Consider the phenomenon of "right-wing women," who believe that women belong in stereotypical roles like that of a housewife and stay-at-home mother even if they prefer other roles, who generally harbor the same attitudes about women as do sexist men, and whose lifestyle largely reflects right-wing values (Superson, 1993a). To be sure, ascertaining whether a woman is a right-wing woman from her behavior and dress is difficult since she might be constrained in her choices or be complicit in patriarchy to get ahead. The question of responsibility arises when we know a person's attitude. Some right-wing women have deformed desires, others simply choose roles that, when enough women choose similarly, perpetuate sexist stereotypes about women which contribute to women's oppression. Are they responsible for not resisting their oppression?

The answers feminists give to the question about responsibility for resisting one's own oppression are responsive to the issue of what best promotes women's agency. Many feminists fully acknowledge women's strong indoctrination into patriarchal beliefs and values and the fact that this makes women likely to endorse them (Bartky, 1999b; Luker, 1984; Nussbaum, 1999a; Superson, 1993a). For example, many Christian women believe that part of God's plan is for women to be subservient to men and their families, and secular right-wing women who understand women's oppression to some extent believe that oppression is unalterable and conformity is their best option. Others simply do not understand, due to strong indoctrination, that women are oppressed, nor do they see how their lifestyle plays a role in their own oppression – consider the Playboy bunny. Some feminists respond that it would be unfair to blame or hold responsible these women: it would be agency-destroying to do so, much like kicking a person who is already down or blaming the victim (Superson, 1993a). Ignorance exonerates them.

Other feminists believe that a more agency-preserving response is that women have an obligation, at least under certain circumstances, to resist their own oppression, even if it is unfair that they do. Perhaps it is true that having deformed desires restricts a woman's autonomy, but that is insufficient reason for not requiring women to resist their own oppression (Hay, 2005). On this view, we can increase women's autonomy when we demand more responsibility of them. In addition, when women carry out their obligation to resist their own oppression, they act in ways that eradicate patriarchy. But we should caution that having an obligation to resist depends on the danger involved, and when the risk of harm to a woman is significant, then she does not have an obligation to resist.

Yet other feminists believe that holding women responsible for resisting their own oppression is not a case of wrongful blaming of the victim, but more like the case of a person who suffers a superficial cut by someone else's careless use of sharp scissors, but who is to blame for some of the harm if he refuses to wash and care for the cut and then loses his hand to gangrene (Cudd, 2006). Both victims are not the initial cause of the harm, though both participate in some way for the harm they suffer. This holds for the case of Lisa and Larry, discussed in Section 2.2.2, where it may be said that Lisa has an obligation to forgo financial benefit for her family, so long as enough other women do the same, to help to overcome the stereotype of women as primarily domestic workers and unreliable wage workers, which causes employers to pay them less than men for the same work. Taking steps to eradicate women's oppression would be agency-affirming.

4 Metaethics

Metaethics means "about" or "beyond" ethics; it presupposes no commitments to particular normative moral theories but goes beyond them and asks questions about ethics itself. It concerns assumptions about ethics that are metaphysical, epistemological, semantic, rational, and psychological in nature. We have already discussed feminist moral psychology in Section 3. Feminists have had little to say about moral semantics, mainly because the topic is done at a highly abstract level that is typically completely independent of gender. We have already discussed in brief the internalism/externalism debate. Feminists have weighed in on truth in ethics, which falls under the realm of metaethics, on how we come to know our moral duties, and on the issue of whether rationality requires that we act morally. Some have worked within the traditional framework of metaethics, while others have questioned this framework. More radical challenges have not yet been made. Along these lines, feminists might question what the point of morality is if actual persons do not follow it in oppressive contexts, and what is the best way to bring about moral progress, instead of focusing on traditional issues such as the meaning of moral terms and moral disagreement. The door is wide open for feminists to explore many different issues that fall under the realm of metaethics rather than the traditional ones.

4.1 Truth in Ethics

According to moral realists, moral claims such as "Woman-abuse is morally wrong" report facts and are true if they get the facts right, and at least some moral claims are actually true (Sayre-McCord, 2015: 1). What is the nature of moral truths? On one view, moral truths are "out there" in the world like other natural properties, or exist in their own world like Platonic facts. We must discover them. On another view, moral truths are given to us through reason, as Hobbes and Kant believed. Since feminism creates new "realities" in the context of social change, it seems to be at odds with the view that moral facts exist independent of humans (Driver, 2012: 175). On the other hand, feminists want it to be the case that it is true that, for instance, woman-abuse is morally wrong. One suggestion for uniting these positions is to adopt a Humean constructivist view of moral realism that is mind-dependent in the sense that the property of being a virtue rests on the feeling of approval in an observer, yet mind-independent in the sense that the moral norms generated are independent of individual and cultural beliefs (Driver, 2012). This complex view is a way to have moral claims such as "Woman-abuse is morally wrong" be true almost universally.

Most of the feminist debate about truth in ethics is not about the nature of moral facts, but about whether feminists should be moral relativists or universalists about truth. Moral relativists believe that truth in ethics is relative to culture or society, while moral universalists believe that there is one true moral code that holds for all people. Moral relativists believe that while it is true in one society that woman-battering is wrong, it might not be true in another society. This does not seem to square with feminism, since if woman-abuse is wrong, it should be universally wrong, given that women are the same kinds of biological beings across cultures. There must be some fact that explains its wrongness which holds for all societies. We can make the same point about women's oppression in general – if it is wrong, it is wrong across the board. Were moral relativism true, feminists would be unable to make these claims about women's oppression, so why would they endorse moral relativism?

The main reason, one held not only by feminists, is the worry that if moral universalism is true, we will judge and be intolerant of other societies and their practices. The worry for feminists in particular stems from a history of judging women according to patriarchal standards. For example, we judge women for being too aggressive, for not putting their family ahead of themselves, and for dressing provocatively. On this view, judging others indicates a failure to understand their position. Indeed, Western feminists have been accused of unfairly judging women in other cultures for being complicit in patriarchy while not saying the same about women in their own culture. Compare veiling women in parts of India to women in the United States who do not go out in public without makeup or with their hairy legs uncovered (Narayan, 2002).

However, this is all to misunderstand moral relativism, since it might be built into a society's moral code that it is morally permissible to judge other cultures and be intolerant. Nothing about moral relativism necessarily precludes judgment or intolerance. Thus, moral relativism does not have this advantage over moral universalism.

Feminists worry about moral universalism as well because it can lead to moral imperialism, which is to say that it can have moral standards grounded in patriarchy that are dictated for everyone. This has led some feminists to endorse multiculturalism, the view that minority cultures should be protected by special group rights and privileges. But other feminists have criticized multiculturalism on the grounds that it can be at odds with the basic tenets of feminism, including that women have human dignity equal to that of men and should have the same opportunities and rights as men (Okin, 2004: 192). These tenets are grounded in an objective, universal standard of value. Feminists criticize practices such as female genital mutilation because it is objectively bad for women in that it causes repeated infections, painful intercourse, obstructed labor and delivery, is irreversible, and is usually forced on females with compromised autonomy such as very young girls and females who are illiterate or poor or intimidated (Nussbaum, 1999b). Feminists have implicitly endorsed moral universalism by taking as obvious that rape, sexual harassment, woman-abuse, and so on are morally wrong, full stop, independent of culture. They have defended the view that date rape is morally wrong because it is not the kind of sex that is reasonable for a woman to consent to because it is noncommunicative and disrespects the woman's desires in the encounter (Pineau, 1989). They have defended the view that rape in general is morally wrong because it is an affront to the victim's value or dignity (Hampton, 1999: 123). Such views point to a universal notion of wrongfulness, even though the expression of certain behaviors counts as wrongful when the behavior fails to conform to what society recognizes as acceptable behavior, and this can vary across cultures. Moral injury itself, being an affront to the victim's dignity, is an objective, not a subjective, injury (Hampton, 1999b: 127). Feminists have defended the wrongness of sexual harassment on objective grounds rather than on subjective feelings of the victim and intentions of the perpetrator as the law does (Superson, 1993b). Such views about the objective wrongness of sexist practices and behavior imply that wrongness is independent of culture.

Finally, some feminists are skeptical about how to defend universal values in a nonpatriarchal, nonpaternalistic way, and for this reason, reject moral universalism. One attempt to defend universalism is the "capabilities theory," according to which we should pursue the fulfillment of central human capabilities that are common to all, thereby treating each person as an end rather than as a tool of the ends of others (Nussbaum, 2000: 5). These capabilities, which when fulfilled promote a good life, include: being able to live to the end of a human life of normal length, to have good health, to have one's bodily boundaries treated as sovereign, to use one's senses, imagination, thought, and reason in ways that produce self-expression, to form a conception of the good and plan one's life critically, and to engage in social interaction and to play (Nussbaum, 2000: 78–80). The idea is to use the objective value of having a good life to judge practices involving women. The practice of woman-abuse would fail the capabilities test at least because the practice violates bodily autonomy and does not promote good health. However, the capabilities theory has been criticized by feminists who remain skeptical that it will not import patriarchal assumptions on behalf of whoever determines whether people's desires are informed, corrupt, or mistaken, since its method is a kind of intuitionism (Jaggar, 2006: 307–8, 318).

Notably, often the explanation for why a sexist act or practice is morally wrong is because it violates autonomy or some important feature of moral agency that allows a person to be a full moral agent. Autonomy is the key feature feminists have seized on – against rape, it is said that women really know what they want when it comes to sex, against woman-abuse, it is said that women should not be held to higher standards of self-defense than men, and so on. Autonomy seems to be a universal value for feminists.

Another factor that might decide whether feminists should be moral relativists or universalists is whether there has been feminist progress. Moral relativists face a challenge in explaining how a society's morality could improve since this seems to require a moral standard that sits outside of that morality against which its progress could be measured. But most feminists believe that we have made feminist progress, though, of course, much more needs to be done to end women's oppression. If they are right, this is reason for feminists to be moral universalists.

4.2 Moral Skepticism

Another issue that feminists have weighed in on is that of "practical moral skepticism," or, the issue of why we should act morally. Suppose that we show what the true moral code is, either for a particular society or for everyone. Moral philosophers want to justify acting on it for both theoretical and practical reasons: demonstrating the rationality of acting morally would strengthen morality by backing it with reason, and good reasons might inspire people to be moved to act morally. The challenge for the moral philosopher is to show that every morally required action is rationally required, and if we show this, no further skeptical challenge remains.

According to the traditional view, the skeptic about the rationality of acting morally adopts a theory of practical reason on which rational action is action that maximizes the agent's expected utility, which is understood to mean the satisfaction of the agent's desires, interests, or preferences. This is called the expected utility theory.

Feminists have challenged the project of defeating the practical skeptic on a variety of fronts. The most radical is to reject the entire project, or at least to reframe it. Some deny that reason could ever be neutral, especially given its association with maleness and the view that reason should conquer "female" emotionality (Held, 1990; Lloyd, 1984). Some care ethicists favor motivating or explanatory reasons rather than justifying reasons for defeating the skeptic, arguing that we should act morally towards our close relatives because we naturally care about and love them. In the case of strangers, we realize that caring is superior to other forms of relatedness and we act morally because we want to live up to the moral ideal (Noddings, 1984: 83, 50). Of course, there are many cases where people lack care about others or about morality so this is not a promising response for those interested in defeating skepticism. Other feminists reject the traditional project of defeating the skeptic because it needs to speak to real people, ones who are not asking for a wholesale defeat of skepticism but who reject or question only pieces of morality (Tessman, 2011: 884). To clarify, the skeptic's position is broadly defined to cover all possible cases of immoral action such that were we to defeat the skeptic, there would be no immoral action about which the skeptic can claim that it is rationally required or at least permissible to act that way.

Along these lines, perhaps the skeptic's position is too narrowly defined since it takes as rational only acts that are self-interested, given their grounding in expected utility theory and the contrast between self-interested and moral action. Feminists want it to be shown that any immoralities that sustain women's oppression, in particular, should be shown to be irrational in a successful defeat of skepticism. These include doing evil for its own sake, displaying moral indifference, moral negligence, conscientious wickedness, and weakness of will, and even benefiting in an undeserved way from an oppressive system (Superson, 2009). A complete defeat of skepticism would demonstrate that all acts that sustain women's oppression are irrational, so it would expand the skeptic's position accordingly. Such acts discount, ignore, or even set back the status of women as full and equal persons. To capture this notion, one proposal is to define the skeptic as endorsing reasons relating to privilege instead of self-interest. Privilege underlies all sexist immoralities, and it means that a person favors their interests and reasons over others and their reasons by failing to respect the intrinsic worth of others, which is inconsistent. Consistency, rather than self-interest, would be the measure of rationality. A successful defeat of skepticism would show that rationality requires, on grounds of consistency, that one not disrespect others' humanity by privileging oneself and one's reasons over another and her reasons (Superson, 2009).

Feminists question whether the expected utility theory of rational choice, which the skeptic is assumed to endorse, is at odds with feminist aims. If it is, it would be a poor starting point for attempting to defeat skepticism. Rational choice theory attempts to explain and predict behavior. Some feminists suggest that in its formal version, it is oblivious to how people form their preferences (Anderson, 2002). This is important for feminists since they acknowledge that people's preferences can be deformed by an unfair social context. The rhetorical version of expected utility theory, which is supposed to explain how people actually behave, has been criticized by some feminists because it takes the rational agent to have characteristic male traits: he knows what he wants and has no unconscious drives that interfere with his conscious desires, takes every opportunity to advance his goals, is resourceful and enterprising, self-reliant, cooly calculating, autonomous, self-confident, and knows his own preferences and sees himself as their source and is ready to assert them (Anderson, 2002: 375–78). The feminist critique of this view of the rational agent is that it is at odds with the agent who cares and is emotionally engaged in a way that is common in intimate interactions like mothering that are associated with women. But other feminists suggest that the "male" model is exactly what we need to counteract stereotypically feminine traits of self-effacement, passivity, servility, and niceness (Anderson, 2002: 378). The male model can be used to measure how women fall short and do not always act on their own preferences, even though this model ignores the social context in which we develop autonomy (Anderson, 2002: 392–93). The male model requires self-interested action that women need a bit more of to counteract socially instilled self-abnegation. Feminists can use traditional rational choice theory to show that it is not rational for women to give care unless doing so is reciprocated (Cudd, 2002: 412–13).

Perhaps a deeper question to ask, one that pulls together this debate about the nature of the rational agent and the role this plays in the position of the skeptic about acting morally, is what we hope to show in defeating skepticism about acting morally. What would an agent who acts morally and thus rationally be like? For purposes of defeating skepticism fully, we want to show that rationality requires acting morally for agents who are rational in the fullest sense. For feminist purposes, we want the fully rational agent to be one whose aims are consistent with feminism.

Two models of the rational agent can be employed to further define the skeptic's position. The Hobbesian model adds the assumption that persons have only instrumental value and that persons who make a hypothetical bargain to arrive at morality may do so in a context that accords them power over their fellows (Superson, 2012: 146). In a patriarchal society, men are in a position of privilege compared to women, and thus have greater instrumental value than women, which gives them more bargaining power. Men would have to weigh the benefits they expect to gain from having a sexist system in place against the benefits they could expect were women not oppressed. The Hobbesian model enables men, due to their social privilege, to privilege themselves and their reasons over others and their reasons. It allows the privileged person to ask, "Why should I participate in a system that requires self-sacrifice?" On this model, the agent is a maximizer about his interests, seeking to satisfy as many of them as possible without driving away other potential bargainers. His goal is to assert his interests, to get as much as possible that would promote his own good in his interactions with others, making concessions only if he can expect to benefit (Superson, 2012: 160).

Feminists criticize the Hobbesian model because it leaves intact systems of oppression. The expected utility theory that it employs faces the additional criticism that it is too thin a view of rational agency since it requires only bare minimum standards for rational action: if you act in ways that best promote your own interest by maximizing the satisfaction of your preferences, you count as rational (Superson, 2012: 162). As we have seen, it has been suggested that even a psychopath can meet this standard of rationality. A psychopath often acts in his own interest, knows what he is doing and does what he wants, and has pro- and con-attitudes toward actions and states of affairs. For purposes of defeating skepticism, we want to best capture what we take to be the ideal rational agent: we want to show that rationality requires acting morally for agents who are rational in the fullest sense. If the agent meets the standard of rational action that a psychopath, who is morally bereft, meets, something important is not captured on this view of rational agency.

An analysis of what is missing in the psychopath can tell us what we need in a fuller account of rational agency. Again, what is lacking in the psychopath are deep emotions, values, and interests, and their logical connection to reasons for action in his own case and in that of others (Cleckley, 1976; Duff, 1977; Nichols, 2002; Superson, 2012:162). The psychopath's emotional impairment impedes his understanding of morality, limiting him to an "inverted commas" understanding that enables him to use the correct moral terms but not to really understand what they mean (Nichols, 2002). The psychopath deliberates instrumentally and often acts self-interestedly, but his behavior is unpredictable. He can see that others have values, such as caring about their family and friends, but he fails to have deep, complex emotions and to see how these values yield reasons for action. Applying this to rational agency, we could surmise that a fuller account of practical reason would not judge an agent's rational status simply by whether she maximizes the satisfaction of her preferences, but by whether the agent has the appropriate emotional attachment to her preferences and understands that this is what links her preferences and those of others to reasons (Superson, 2012: 163). Crucial for ideal rational agency is that the agent be self-determining. The interest-asserting model goes some way toward this since acting on one's own interests allows the agent to develop by asserting one's interests and to grow through cultivating new interests, but only if one cares appropriately about one's interests. External impediments that constrain women need to be removed so that women can be interest-asserting in the way men are (Superson, 2012: 164).

A different, Kantian model of rational agency, one that favors protecting one's interests, is also essential for self-determination. Kant's Universal Law Formulation requires that the agent ask whether he can will – both imagine and want – a maxim to be a universal law. The agent does not take a self-interested perspective but must imagine what he would will when his circumstances have changed in such a way that when others aim to satisfy their desires, he might end up in a position that he would not want, a desire that conflicts with the desire he would fulfill were only he to act on the maxim. Kantian rationality invokes consistency: if in willing a maxim to be a universal law the agent runs into a contradiction in his desires, rationality requires rejecting the maxim as one we ought to follow. The Principle of Autonomy takes things a step further, requiring that the agent actually take the perspective of the nonprivileged. It asks whether anyone else would consent to a maxim, absent coercion and deception, that the agent wants that would serve his own ends. An agent would not will a maxim that would give him the short end of the stick by not respecting his worth as a person, and would see, on pains of inconsistency, that no one else would will a maxim that would give them the short end of the stick. The agent defers to morality, being constrained by whether others would agree to his acting on certain reasons that reflect his preferences. His goal is to protect himself from being taken advantage of or from having his humanity disrespected and doing the same for any other rational being. He defends his interests against invasion, as it were. Universalization helps the agent become aware that she has desires or interests that she cares about appropriately, and autonomy ensures that she cares enough about her interests to protect them from being set back in ways to which she would not autonomously consent. She recognizes that everyone else cares about their own interests too.

The feminist suggestion is to change the notion of ideal rational agency to be more robust than that found in expected utility theory. Robust rational agency requires more than being interest-maximizing. It requires also that the agent has the appropriate attachment to her preferences and understands that this is what links her preferences and those of others to reasons. The ideal rational agent makes a real choice about whether reason dictates following morality or self-interest or any other way of acting immorally. Instead of asking what is in it for me when it comes to morally required action, the agent asks, "Given that I have intrinsic value and that I am able to protect and assert my interests because I care appropriately about them, what kind of action is rationally required?" (Superson, 2012: 165). The answer promises to be more robust than the one given by the agent who merely wants to know what's in it for him to act morally.

4.3 Moral Epistemology

Moral epistemology is the issue of how we come to know our moral duties. The traditional view espoused by many moral theories is that reason determines our duties, we are motivated when we acknowledge our duties, and motivation prompts action. Many traditional moral theorists reject the view that emotion plays a role in determining duty because they suspect that it will introduce bias. Feminists take issue with this view, agreeing with the care ethicists' suspicion that emotion has been downplayed due to its historical association with women. On this view, not only should emotion play a role in determining our duties, but it is necessary for our coming to know the moral landscape (Little, 2007: 421). This is to say that emotions such as care, concern, love, anger, revulsion, and indignation, are essential for knowing what is morally called for in a situation and for getting us to moral truths (Little, 2007: 421). In particular, care about people, not just care about an impersonal moral end such as justice, is necessary for determining the requirements of morality (Little, 2007: 421). When we care about a person, we have the right background disposition for morally relevant features to come into our consciousness, allowing us to pick up on which details are morally salient. Consider the good mother who can tell when her child needs a little extra attention, and the loving daughter who knows that her mother wants to be clean before bedtime and pays a return visit each evening to the nursing home to brush her teeth and wash her face. Caring makes us receptive to the particularities of a person, enables us to listen to their narrative, including their fears, hopes, and worries, and makes us respect the person as a responsible subject with whom we even can disagree (Little, 2007: 423–25). Trying to learn our duties dispassionately would make us less likely to pick up on what is morally salient and more likely to miss what our duties are.

Indeed, those who have merely an intellectual comprehension of the moral landscape but never respond appropriately have a clouded perception. They are like the person who uses the term "green" correctly but has never seen the color and so lacks the concept of "green" (Little, 2007: 427). Consider the person who sees that certain things are painful and knows what pain is yet does not see pain as evil and that we have a reason not to cause pain (Little, 2007: 425–26). This person does not get morality right for two reasons. One is that nonmoral terms like "pain" cannot completely explain morality – for instance, they cannot explain the difference in the cruelty of kicking a dog, picking on a child, and refusing to get groceries for someone when that has been your practice. Each of these acts is painful but in different ways that we need emotion to grasp. Second, whether a feature of an act plays a role in determining the act's moral status is dependent, in a way that cannot be codified, on other relevant features.

For example, an act's being fun may serve as a reason to do it, but it is also a feature that makes hunting animals morally problematic (Little, 2007: 428). Emotion explains the difference. Thus, care and other affections, not reason alone, can get us to moral truths, and are necessary for doing so.

These insights about care are significant not only for moral epistemology but also for moral agency. According to many justice theories of morality, the ideal moral agent is one who follows the rules the theory mandates. For Hobbes, one should follow the rule about acting in ways that best promote one's self-interest, for utilitarians, one should follow the rule about promoting the general welfare, and for Kant, one should follow the Categorical Imperative. From this list, motivation is important mostly for Kant, who argues that, for one's act to have moral worth, it should be done from the moral motive, which is a rational motive that has duty as its content. On any of these theories, the agent first ascertains what their duty is, then engages the appropriate motive. The view that care is essential for even determining one's duties suggests that care allows the agent to understand a much more nuanced view of morality than is typical for justice theories that offer general rules of guidance. This bears on moral agency in that the ideal moral agent comes to know morality in its fullest, nuanced sense through care and other emotions. Moral agency would not consist in mere rule-following even when following the rule is accompanied by the moral motive; rather, robust moral agency involves acquiring a certain sensitivity that allows the agent to perceive the nuances of duty and then to act appropriately. The care model provides a richer view of morality, and a richer account of moral agency, than the justice model. The agent can be a better moral person if she sees morality in its fullest sense and acts on it. We can all agree that this is an important aim of morality.

5 Conclusion

Feminist philosophers have enriched traditional morality, in normative theory, moral psychology, metaethics, and applied ethics. Their insistence that morality attend to emotion, to oppression and its effect on moral agents, and to the ways that traditional questions in ethics need to reflect social context have led them to defend a richer view of both moral theory and moral agency. While they have already made a huge contribution to ethics, they have left ethics wide open for further exploration along feminist lines. This exploration promises to give us the best answers to the pressing questions of how we should act and what kind of persons we should become.

References

Anderson, E. (2002). Should Feminists Reject Rational Choice Theory? In L. M. Antony & C. E. Witt, eds., 2nd ed., *A Mind of One's Own: Feminist Essays on Reason and Objectivity*. Boulder, CO: Westview Press, pp. 369–97.

Asefa, S. (1998). Female Genital Mutilation: Violence in the Name of Tradition, Religion, and Social Imperative. In S. G. French, W. Teays, & L. M. Purdy, eds., *Violence Against Women: Philosophical Perspectives*. Ithaca, NY: Cornell University Press, pp. 92–104.

Baber, H. (2007). Adaptive Preference. *Social Theory and Practice*, 33(1), 105–26.

Baier, A. (1987). The Need for More Than Justice. *Canadian Journal of Philosophy*, 13(Supplement), 41–56.

Bailey, A. (1998). Privilege: Expanding on Marilyn Frye's "Oppression." *Journal of Social Philosophy*, 29(3), 104–19.

Barnhill, A. (2012). Modesty as a Feminist Virtue. In S. L. Crasnow & A. M. Superson, eds., *Out from the Shadows: Analytical Feminist Contributions to Traditional Philosophy*. New York: Oxford University Press, pp. 115–37.

Bartky, S. (1990a). Narcissism, Femininity, and Alienation. In S. L. Bartky, ed., *Femininity and Domination: Studies in the Phenomenology of Oppression*. New York: Routledge, pp. 33–44.

Bartky, S. (1999b). On Psychological Oppression. In S. L. Bartky, ed., *Femininity and Domination: Studies in the Phenomenology of Oppression*. New York: Routledge, pp. 22–32.

Beneke, T. (1997). *Proving Manhood: Reflections on Men and Sexism*, Berkeley, CA: University of California Press.

Benson, P. (2000). Feeling Crazy: Self-Worth and the Social Character of Responsibility. In C. Mackenzie & N. Stoljar, eds., *Relational Autonomy: Feminist Perspectives on Autonomy, Agency, and the Social Self*. New York: Oxford University Press, pp. 72–93.

Bettcher, T. M. (2007). Evil Deceivers and Make-Believers: On Transphobic Violence and the Politics of Illusion. *Hypatia*, 22(3), 43–65.

Blum, L. (1988). Gilligan and Kohlberg: Implications for Moral Theory. *Ethics*, 98(3), 472–91.

Blum, L., Homiak, M., Housman, J., and Scheman, N. et. al. (1973–1974). Altruism and Women's Oppression. *The Philosophical Forum: Special Issue on Women & Philosophy*, 5(1–2), 222–47.

Bordo, S. (1997). Can a Woman Harass a Man? *Philosophy Today*, 4(1), 51–66.

Brink, D. (1986). Externalist Moral Realism. *The Southern Journal of Philosophy*, 24 (Supplement), 23–41.

Brison, S. (1993). Outliving Oneself: Trauma, Memory, and Personal Identity. In D. T. Meyers, ed., *Feminists Rethink the Self*. New York: Taylor & Francis, pp. 12–39.

Brison, S. J. (1998). Surviving Sexual Violence: A Philosophical Perspective. In S. G. French, W. Teays, & L. M. Purdy, eds., *Violence against Women: Philosophical Perspectives*. Ithaca: Cornell University Press, pp. 11–26.

Bruckner, D. W. (2007). In Defense of Adaptive Preferences. *Philosophical Studies*, 142, 307–24.

Buss, S. (1997). Justified Wrongdoing. *Nous*, 31(3), 337–69.

Caldwell, P. M. (1991). A Hair Piece: Perspectives on the Intersection of Race and Gender. *Duke Law Journal*, 1(2), 365–96.

Calhoun, C. (1988). Justice, Care, and Gender Bias. *The Journal of Philosophy*, 85(9), 451–63.

Calhoun, C. (1989). Responsibility and Reproach. *Ethics*, 99(2), 389–406.

Calhoun, C. (2004). Introduction. In C. Calhoun, ed., *Setting the Moral Compass: Essays by Women Philosophers*. New York: Oxford University Press, pp. 3–19.

Card, C. (1993). Gender and Moral Luck. In O. J. Flanagan & A. Oksenberg, eds., *Identity, Character, and Morality: Essays in Moral Psychology*. Bradford, MA: MIT University Press, pp. 199–218.

Cleckley, H. (1976). *The Mask of Sanity: An Attempt to Clarify Some Issues about the So-Called Psychopathic Personality*, 5th ed., St. Louis: Mosby.

Copp, D. (1982). Harman on Internalism, Relativism, and Logical Form. *Ethics*, 92(2), 227–42.

Crenshaw, K. (1989). Demarginalizing the Intersection of Race and Sex: A Black Feminist Critique of Antidiscrimination Doctrine, Feminist Theory and Antiracist Politics. *University of Chicago Legal Forum*, 1, 139–67.

Cudd, A. E. (1988). Oppression by Choice. *Journal of Social Philosophy*, 25, 22–44.

Cudd, A. E. (1990). Enforced Pregnancy, Rape, and the Image of Woman. *Philosophical Studies*, 60, 45–59.

Cudd, A. E. (2002). Rational Choice Theory and the Lessons of Feminism. In L. M. Antony & C. E. Witt, eds., *A Mind of One's Own: Feminist Essays on Reason and Objectivity*, 2nd ed. Boulder, CO: Westview Press, pp. 398–417.

Cudd, A. E. (2006). *Analyzing Oppression*, New York: Oxford University Press.

Daly, M. (1978). *Gyn/Ecology: The Metaethics of Radical Feminism*, Boston, MA: Beacon Press.

DesAutels, P. (2004). Moral Mindfulness. In P. Des Autels & M. A. Walker, eds., *Moral Psychology: Feminist Ethics and Social Theory*. Lanham, MD: Rowman & Littlefield, pp. 69–81.

Descartes, R. (1979). *Meditations of First Philosophy*, D. A. Cress, trans., Indianapolis: Hackett.

Digby, T. (2011). *Love and War: How Militarism Shapes Sexuality and Romance*, New York: Columbia University Press.

Dillon, R. S. (2012). Critical Character Theory: Toward a Feminist Perspective on "Vice"(and "Virtue"). In S. L. Crasnow & A. M. Superson, eds., *Out from the Shadows: Analytical Feminist Contributions to Traditional Philosophy*. New York: Oxford University Press, pp. 83–114.

Driver, J. (2012). Constructivism and Feminism. In S. L. Crasnow & A. M. Superson, eds., *Out from the Shadows: Analytical Feminist Contributions to Traditional Philosophy*. New York: Oxford University Press, pp. 175–94.

Duff, A. (1977). Psychopathy and Moral Understanding. *American Philosophical Quarterly*, 14(3), 189–200.

Dworkin, A. (1987). *Intercourse*, New York: Free Press.

Estrich, S. (1993). Rape. In P. Smith, ed., *Feminist Jurisprudence*. New York: Oxford University Press, pp. 158–87.

Flanagan, O. & Jackson, K. (1987). Justice, Care, and Gender: The Kohlberg-Gilligan Debate Revisited. *Ethics*, 97(3), 622–37.

Friedman, M. A. (1985). Moral Integrity and the Deferential Wife. *Philosophical Studies*, 47(1), 141–50.

Friedman, M. (1993). Liberating Care. In M. Friedman (ed.) *What Are Friends For?* Ithaca, NY: Cornell University Press, pp. 142-83.

Frye, M. (1983). Oppression. In M. Frye, ed., *The Politics of Reality: Essays in Feminist Theory*. Trumansburg, NY: Crossing, pp. 1–16.

Frye, M. (1995). White Woman Feminist. In C. Koggel, ed., *Moral Issues in Global Perspectives*. Peterborough: Broadview Press, pp. 224–39.

Garry, A. (2012). Who Is Included? Intersectionality, Metaphors, and the Multiplicity of Gender. In S. L. Crasnow & A. M. Superson, eds., *Out from the Shadows: Analytical Feminist Contributions to Traditional Philosophy*. New York: Oxford University Press, pp. 493–530.

Gilligan, C. (1982). *In a Different Voice: Psychological Theory and Women's Development*, Cambridge, MA: Harvard University Press.

Gilligan, C. (1987). Moral Orientation and Moral Development. In E. Kittay & D. T. Meyers, eds., *Women and Moral Theory*. New York: Rowman and Littlefield Publishers, pp. 19–33.

Gilligan, J. (1997). *Violence: Reflections on a National Epidemic*, New York: Vintage Books.

Grasswick, H. E. (2012). Knowing Moral Agents: Epistemic Dependence and the Moral Realm. In S. L. Crasnow & A. M. Superson, eds., *Out from the Shadows: Analytical Feminist Contributions to Traditional Philosophy*. New York: Oxford University Press, pp. 37–38.

Greeno, C. G. & Maccoby, E. E. (1993). How Different Is the "Different Voice?" In M. J. Larrabee, ed., *An Ethic of Care: Feminist and Interdisciplinary Perspectives*. New York: Routledge, pp. 222–47.

Griffin, S. (1981). Rape: The All-American Crime. In M. Vetterling-Braggin, F. A. Elliston, & J. English, eds., *Feminism and Philosophy*. Totowa, NJ: Littlefield, Adams, pp. 313–32.

Hampton, J. (1999). Defining Wrong and Defining Rape. In K. Burgess-Jackson, ed., *A Most Detestable Crime*. New York: Oxford University Press, pp. 118–56.

Hampton, J. (2002). Feminist Contractarianism. In L. M. Antony & C. E. Witt, eds., *A Mind of One's Own: Feminist Essays on Reason and Objectivity*, 2nd ed. Boulder, CO: Westview Press, pp. 337–68.

Harman, G. (1975). Moral Relativism Defended. *Philosophical Review*, 84(1), 3–22.

Harvey, J. (1999). *Civilized Oppression*, Lanham, MD: Rowman and Littlefield.

Hay, C. (2005). Whether to Ignore Them and Spin: Moral Obligations to Resist Sexual Harassment. *Hypatia: A Journal of Feminist Philosophy*, 20(4), 94–108.

Held, V. (1990). Feminist Transformations of Moral Theory. *Philosophy and Phenomenological Research*, 1, 321–44.

Held, V. (2006). *The Ethics of Care: Personal, Political, and Global*, New York: Oxford University Press.

Herman, B. (1981). On the Value of Acting from the Motive of Duty. *Philosophical Review*, 90(3), 359–82.

Hill, T. E., Jr. (1995). Servility and Self-Respect. In R. S. Dillon, ed., *Dignity, Character, and Self-Respect*. New York: Routledge, pp. 76–92.

Hoagland, S. L. (1991). Some Thoughts about "Caring." In C. Card, ed., *Feminist Ethics*. Lawrence, KS: University of Kansas Press, pp. 246–63.

Hobbes, T. (1962). *Leviathan*, M. Oakeshott, ed., New York: Collier Books.

Isaacs, T. (2011). *Moral Responsibility in Collective Contexts*, New York: Oxford University Press.

Jaggar, A. (1983). *Feminist Politics and Human Nature*. Totowa, NJ: Rowman & Allanheld.

Jaggar, A. M. (2001). Feminist Ethics. In L. Becker, ed., *Encyclopedia of Ethics*. New York: Routledge, pp. 528–39.

Jaggar, A. M. (2006). Reasoning about Well-Being: Nussbaum's Methods of Justifying. *Journal of Political Philosophy*, 14(3), 301–22.

Kant, I. (1981). *Grounding for the Metaphysics of Morals*, J. W. Ellington, trans., Indianapolis: Hackett.

Khader, S. J. (2011). *Adaptive Preferences and Women's Empowerment*, New York: Oxford University Press.

Kittay, E. F. (1999). *Love's Labor: Essays on Women, Equality, and Dependency*, New York: Routledge.

Korsgaard, C. M. (1986). Skepticism about Practical Reason. *The Journal of Philosophy*, 83(1), 5–25.

Langton, R. (2009). Autonomy-Denial in Objectification. In R. Langton, ed., *Sexual Solipsism: Philosophical Essays on Pornography and Objectification*. New York: Oxford University Press, pp. 223–40.

Little, M. O. (2007). Seeing and Caring: The Role of Affect in Feminist Moral Epistemology. In R. Shafer-Landau & T. Cuneo, eds., *Foundations of Ethics: An Anthology*. Malden, MA: Blackwell, pp. 420–32.

Lloyd, G. (1984). *The Man of Reason: "Male" and "Female" in Western Philosophy*, Minneapolis, MN: University of Minnesota Press.

Lugones, M. (1995). Playfulness, "World"-Traveling, and Loving Perception. In K. Mehuron & G. Percesepe, eds., *Free Spirits: Feminist Philosophers on Culture*. New Jersey: Prentice-Hall, pp. 121–28.

Luker, K. (1984). *Abortion and the Politics of Motherhood*, Berkeley: University of California Press.

Luria, Z. (1993). A Methodological Critique. In M. J. Larrabee, ed., *An Ethic of Care: Feminist and Interdisciplinary Perspectives*. New York: Routledge, pp. 199–203.

Mackenzie, C. (2001). On Bodily Autonomy. In S. K. Toombs, ed., *Handbook of Phenomenology and Medicine*. The Netherlands: Kluwer Academic, pp. 417–39.

Mackenzie, C. & Stoljar, N. (2000). Introduction: Autonomy Refigured. In C. Mackenzie & N. Stoljar, eds., *Relational Autonomy: Feminist Perspectives on Autonomy, Agency, and the Social Self*. New York: Oxford University Press, pp. 3–31.

MacKinnon, C. (1987). Difference and Dominance: On Sex Discrimination. In C. MacKinnon, ed., *Feminism Unmodified: Discourses on Life and Law*. Cambridge, MA: Harvard University Press, pp. 32–45.

May, L. (1998). Socialization and Separatism. In L. May, ed., *Masculinity and Morality*. Ithaca, NY: Cornell University Press, pp. 116–34.

May, L. & Strikwerda, R. (1994). Men in Groups: Collective Responsibility for Rape. *Hypatia*, 9(2), 134–51.

McDowell, J. (1978). Are Moral Requirements Hypothetical Imperatives? *Proceedings of the Aristotelian Society, Supplementary Volume*, 52, 13–29.

McDowell, J. (1979). Virtue and Reason. *The Monist*, 62(3), 331–50.

McIntosh, P. (1993). White Privilege and Male Privilege. In A. Minas, ed., *Gender Basics: Feminist Perspectives on Women and Men*. Belmont, CA: Wadsworth, pp. 30–38.

Menkiti, I. A. (1977–78). The Resentment of Injustice: Some Consequences of Institutional Racism. *The Philosophical Forum*, 9(2–3), 227–49.

Mill, J. S. (1978). *On Liberty*, Indianapolis, IN: Hackett.

Mill, J. S. & Mill, H. T. (1869)(Written 1861). *The Subjection of Women*, London: Longmans, Green, Reader & Dyer.

Mills, C. (2005). "Ideal Theory" as Ideology. *Hypatia*, 20(3), 165–84.

Moody-Adams, M. (1994). Culture, Responsibility, and Affected Ignorance. *Ethics*, 104(2), 291–309.

Narayan, U. (2002). Minds of Their Own: Choices, Autonomy, Cultural Practices, and Other Women. In L. M. Antony & C. E. Witt, eds., 2nd ed., *A Mind of One's Own: Feminist Essays on Reason and Objectivity*. Boulder, CO: Westview Press, pp. 418–32.

Nichols, S. (2002). How Psychopaths Threaten Moral Rationalism. *The Monist*, 85(2), 285–303.

Noddings, N. (1984). *Caring: A Feminine Approach to Ethics and Moral Education*, Berkeley: University of California Press.

Nussbaum, M. C. (1999a). American Women. In M. C. Nussbaum, ed., *Sex and Social Justice*. New York: Oxford University Press, pp. 130–53.

Nussbaum, M. C. (1999b). Judging Other Cultures: The Case of Genital Mutilation. In M. C. Nussbaum, ed., *Sex and Social Justice*. New York: Oxford University Press, pp. 118–29.

Nussbaum, M. C. (2000). *Women and Human Development: The Capabilities Approach*, New York: Cambridge University Press.

Okin, S. M. (2004). Is Multiculturalism Bad for Women? In A. Baehr, ed., *Varieties of Feminist Liberalism*. Lanham, MD: Rowman & Littlefield, pp. 191–205.

Pineau, L. (1989). Date Rape: A Feminist Analysis. *Law and Philosophy*, 8, 217–43.

Railton, P. (1984). Alienation, Consequentialism, and Morality. *Philosophy & Public Affairs*, 13(2), 134–71.

Ruddick, S. (1980). Maternal Thinking. In M. Persall, ed., *Women and Values: Readings in Recent Feminist Philosophy*. Belmont, CA: Wadsworth, pp. 340–51.

Sayre-McCord, G. (2015). Moral Realism. In E. Zalta, ed., *The Stanford Encyclopedia of Philosophy*, Spring ed. http://plato.stanford.edu/archives/spr2015/entries/moral-realism/.

Smith, M. (1994). *The Moral Problem*, Malden, MA: Blackwell.

Stark, C. A. (1997). The Rationality of Valuing Oneself: A Critique of Kant on Self-Respect. *Journal of the History of Philosophy*, 35(1), 65–82.

Stocker, M. (1976). The Schizophrenia of Modern Moral Theories. *The Journal of Philosophy*, 73(14), 453–66.

Stoljar, N. (2000). Autonomy and the Feminist Intuition. In C. Mackenzie & N. Stoljar, eds., *Relational Autonomy: Feminist Perspectives on Autonomy, Agency, and the Social Self*. New York: Oxford University Press, pp. 94–123.

Superson, A. M. (1993a). Right-Wing Women Causes, Choices, and Blaming the Victim. *Journal of Social Philosophy*, 73(14), 453–66.

Superson, A. M. (1993b). A Feminist Definition of Sexual Harassment. *Journal of Social Philosophy*, 24(1), 46–64.

Superson, A. M. (2004). Privilege, Immorality, and Responsibility for Attending to the Facts about Humanity. *Journal of Social Philosophy*, 35(1), 34–55.

Superson, A. M. (2009). *The Moral Skeptic*, New York: Oxford University Press.

Superson, A. M. (2010). The Deferential Wife Revisited: Agency, Responsibility, and Self-Respect. *Hypatia: A Journal of Feminist Philosophy*, 25(2), 253–75.

Superson, A. M. (2012). Standards of Rationality and the Challenge of the Moral Skeptic. In S. L. Crasnow & A. M. Superson, eds., *Out from the Shadows: Analytical Feminist Contributions to Traditional Philosophy*. New York: Oxford University Press, pp. 139–73.

Superson, A. M. (2014). The Right to Bodily Autonomy and the Abortion Controversy. In A. Veltman & M. Piper, eds., *Autonomy, Oppression, and Gender*. New York: Oxford University Press, pp. 301–25.

Teays, W. (1998). Standards of Perfection and Battered Women's Self-defense. In S. G. French, W. Teays, & L. M. Purdy, eds., *Violence against Women: Philosophical Perspectives*. Ithaca, NY: Cornell University Press, pp. 57–76.

Tessman, L. (2001). Critical Virtue Ethics: Understanding Oppression as Morally Damaging. In P. DesAutels & J. Waugh, eds., *Feminists Doing Ethics*. Lanham, MD: Rowman & Littlefield, pp. 79–99.

Tessman, L. (2005). *Burdened Virtues: Virtue Ethics for Liberatory Struggles*, New York: Routledge.

Tessman, L. (2011). Book Review of *The Moral Skeptic*, by Anita Superson. *Hypatia: A Journal of Feminist Philosophy*, 26(4), 883–87.

Thomas, L. (1999). Moral Deference. In C. Koggel, ed., *Moral Issues in Global Perspectives*. Peterborough: Broadview Press, pp. 180–91.

Thomson, J. J. (1971). A Defense of Abortion. *Philosophy & Public Affairs*, 1(1), 47–66.

Tronto, J. (1993). Beyond Gender Difference to a Theory of Care. In M. J. Larrabee, ed., *An Ethic of Care: Feminist and Interdisciplinary Perspectives*. New York: Routledge, pp. 240–57.

Tuana, N. (1992). *Women and the History of Philosophy*, New York: Paragon House.

Varden, H. (2012). A Feminist, Kantian Conception of the Right to Bodily Integrity: The Cases of Abortion and Homosexuality. In S. L. Crasnow & A. M. Superson, eds., *Out from the Shadows: Analytical Feminist Contributions to Traditional Philosophy*. New York: Oxford University Press, pp. 33–57.

Waits, K. (1993). The Criminal Justice System's Response to Battering: Understanding the Problem, Forging the Solutions. In P. Smith, ed., *Feminist Jurisprudence*. New York: Oxford University Press, pp. 188–209.

Walker, L. J. (1993). Sex Differences in the Development of Moral Reasoning: A Critical Review. In M. J. Larrabee, ed., *An Ethic of Care: Feminist and Interdisciplinary Perspectives*. New York: Routledge, pp. 157–76.

Westlund, A. C. (2003). Selflessness and Responsibility for Self: Is Deference Compatible with Autonomy? *The Philosophical Review*, 112(4), 483–523.

Wilson, C. (2004). The Preferences of Women. In P. Desautels & M. U. Walker, eds., *Moral Psychology: Feminist Ethics and Social Theory*. Lanham, MD: Rowman & Littlefield, pp. 99–117.

Wolf, N. (1992). *The Beauty Myth: How Images of Beauty Are Used against Women*, New York: Anchor Books.

Wolf, S. (1986). Asymmetrical Freedom. In J. M. Fischer, ed., *Moral Responsibility*. Ithaca, NY: Cornell University Press, pp. 225–40.

Young, I. (1988). Five Faces of Oppression. *Philosophical Forum*, 19(4), 270–90.

Zack, N. (1998). *Thinking about Race*, Belmont, CA: Wadsworth.

Cambridge Elements⁼

Ethics

Ben Eggleston

University of Kansas

Ben Eggleston is a professor of philosophy at the University of Kansas. He is the editor of John Stuart Mill, *Utilitarianism: With Related Remarks from Mill's Other Writings* (Hackett, 2017) and a co-editor of *Moral Theory and Climate Change: Ethical Perspectives on a Warming Planet* (Routledge, 2020), *The Cambridge Companion to Utilitarianism* (Cambridge, 2014), and *John Stuart Mill and the Art of Life* (Oxford, 2011). He is also the author of numerous articles and book chapters on various topics in ethics.

Dale E. Miller

Old Dominion University, Virginia

Dale E. Miller is a professor of philosophy at Old Dominion University. He is the author of *John Stuart Mill: Moral, Social and Political Thought* (Polity, 2010) and a co-editor of *Moral Theory and Climate Change: Ethical Perspectives on a Warming Planet* (Routledge, 2020), *A Companion to Mill* (Blackwell, 2017), *The Cambridge Companion to Utilitarianism* (Cambridge, 2014), *John Stuart Mill and the Art of Life* (Oxford, 2011), and *Morality, Rules, and Consequences: A Critical Reader* (Edinburgh, 2000). He is also the editor-in-chief of *Utilitas*, and the author of numerous articles and book chapters on various topics in ethics broadly construed.

About the Series

This Elements series provides an extensive overview of major figures, theories, and concepts in the field of ethics. Each entry in the series acquaints students with the main aspects of its topic while articulating the author's distinctive viewpoint in a manner that will interest researchers.